Is It Monday Yet?

Is It Monday Yet?

A poetry anthology celebrating Monday Night Poetry

edited by Jesse James Ziegler, Mackensi Green, & Eric Morago

~ 2026 ~

Is It Monday Yet?
© Copyright 2026
All rights reserved and revert back to the individual authors. No part of this book may be used or reproduced in any manner whatsoever without written permission from either the author or the publisher, except in the case of credited epigraphs or brief quotations embedded in articles or reviews.

Moon Tide Press Editor-in-chief
Eric Morago

Anthology Editors
Jesse James Ziegler
Mackensi Green
Eric Morago

Operations Associate
Shelly Holder

Moon Tide Press Associate Editors
Mackensi Green
Ellen Webre
Allysa Murray

Editor Emeritus
Michael Miller

Front cover art
Rachel Grey

Book design
Michael Wada

Moon Tide logo design
Abraham Gomez

Is It Monday Yet?
is published by Moon Tide Press

Moon Tide Press
6709 Washington Ave. #9297
Whittier, CA 90608
www.moontidepress.com

FIRST EDITION

Printed in the United States of America

ISBN #978-1-9557799-48-3

Next up on the microphone...

Where they at?
Where they at?
Where they at?

Contents

Foreword by Jesse James Ziegler — 14

Isis Atkins
   10 Things to Do Before the World Ends — 17
Sammy Aucella
   Porcelain and Prayer — 19
Ms. AyeVee
   Sticky Hands — 22
Latreece Bass
   Persistence — 23
M. Colton Brodeur
   The Atronach — 24
Derrick C. Brown
   Waltzing the Hurricane — 26
Alon Burton
   Shapeshifter — 29
Elisa Carlsen
   Dear Mark Twain, — 31
Scoot Carnahan
   My Dog Has Nipples — 32
   Savage Cute Bastard — 35
Andrew Coffey
   The House is Burning — 38
Shelby Contreras
   CC and Cheap Wine — 40
Camilla Downs
   Tilt — 41
Natalia Durán
   Ella (She Is the Moon) — 44
Erin Eddings
   Jesus was... an Elephant... Never Forgets — 46
Steve Elegant
   Mourning Breaths — 48
Fia Ewers
   The Way in Which I Will Live — 49

Jean-Aléx Fonvil
    WE   50

Dominique Frida Francis
    The Gospel According to Eve   53

Elisa Garcia
    Gold Hoops   55
    The Garcia Girls   57

Anna Glenn
    The Miracle is Already Here   59

Mackensi Green
    Ghost Hunting   62

Rachel Grey
    I Carry Home   63

Nikki Leialohalani Herschend
    A Lion, A Saber, and A Crown   64

Priya Hutner
    Unspoken   68

Sophia Jacobson
    Her Masterpiece   72

Levi Johnson
    Like an Occultist   74

Samantha Jones
    Am I Porn Yet?   76

Trevor Owen Jones
    Luck and Its Torments   78

Britt Keehn
    A History of Displacement   79

Courtney Kelly
    The Ginko   81
    Cratered When We Kiss   83

Brandon Leake
    Dear Daniel   84

Anthony Lomando
    Nassir   87

Aimee Lowenstern
    Poet's Envy   90

John Merryfield
    The Shining Path (El Sendero Luninoso)   92

Eric Morago
    When They Told You It Was Them and Not You   93
    (But Really It Was You)
    Lies I Tell My Therapist   95

Pan Pantoja
    Transmission   97

Griffin Peralta
    Live Ammunition   99

Melanie Perish
    Apparition at the Edge of the World   101

Atticus Pizzo
    Rally Cry   102

Dani Putney
    Explorers of Darkness   106
    List of Suitors   108

Pax Robinson
    Find Another Way   110

Jason Sarna
    First Day   112
    God, Family, Country   116

Chris Warren Smith
    Walk to Eternity   118

Raymond Solorzano
    What is Burning Man?   119

Baylee Moon Spear
    I Am a Doll   122

Larissa Storm
    Van Gogh   126

Cheyenne Scott Taylor
    In Your Room, God Is Easy   128

Karen A. Terrey
    Three-Legged Horses   133

Em Tomeo
    A Dog Still Loves You After You Beat It   135

TWOSHAE
    Exclamation   137

Logan Veith
    More Than I Can Carry   138

Iain Watson
    Black & Blue   140
    My Love   143
Coley Whisman
    Rebuttal to Your Salty Love Poem   147
Jesse James Ziegler
    Squint   151
    Keep   155

Afterword by Eric Morago   *156*
About the Editors   *158*

*If we have nothing
but each other
we have so much*

— Andrea Gibson

Foreword

It is a vulnerably brave thing to share with a roomful of strangers and chosen family from our innermost being. It is deeply cathartic and revelatory too. On January 3rd, 2022 Monday Night Poetry was revealed to the public for the very first time in the heart of downtown for the Biggest Little City in the World. Since then, the art form of poetry has been celebrated as a written and oral tradition on a weekly basis. Poets from all over the country have graced the built-in stage at Shim's Tavern and locals have co-created a distinct and vibrant community surrounding the special event within the greater Truckee Meadows region.

It all started with a desire by Zach Cage to encourage a bustling environment and drum up business for the speakeasy on nights of the week which weren't traditionally as busy. He reached out to Oliver X (may he forever rest in power as a creative icon and artist friend to countless souls). Oliver in turn reached out to Iain Watson, founder of Spoken Views Collective in 2006 and co-founder of MNP, to see about the prospect of creating a recurring open mic event towards the beginning of the average work week. This is where I came in. An in-person meeting towards the end of 2021 between Zach, Iain, and I changed the trajectory of the entire poetry scene in western Nevada from that point forward.

The world was seemingly coming out of Covid hibernation and desperate for deep, rich, meaningful connection with other human beings that wasn't attempting to pass through a digital screen as an intermediary. In person gatherings were becoming more widely accepted again. Venues were opening back up more substantially, and creatives were hungry for entities which fed their spirits in ways that Zoom meetings couldn't.

The single greatest feeling this life has to offer us is being a part of something that is larger than just ourselves. Poetry is the language of grieving and of healing. It is a conduit for social activism and personal revelation. It brings together academic aficionados from the universities and powerful street performers with raw open messages to deliver. It welcomes beginners and seasoned professionals. It holds space for marginalized voices and widely embraced ones.

I wanted to help create something I personally longed for, something special and lasting, which would build and serve the community in a greater capacity than any single individual can do on their own. It has been my greatest joy to realize how many others would be willing to come alongside the efforts and consistently fill the space between the walls at 125 W 3rd St in Reno, Nevada with warmth, safety, artistic integrity and an unmatched welcoming of strangers who become friends.

Friends like Mackensi Green and Eric Morago.

I first met Mackensi at the Laughing Planet Cafe beside The University of Nevada Reno. She was reading her poetry at the monthly Brushfire Literary Arts Journal open mic, and I immediately knew she was going places in this world. Captivating. Heartfelt and deeply raw. In time, I had the honor of writing her a letter of recommendation for graduate school, which allows me to live vicariously through her as she pursues her MFA at NYU.

Eric and I crossed paths at an event I was hosting within the annual Mark Twain Days in Carson City, Nevada. I am eternally grateful to him and his publishing house, Moon Tide Press, for the glorious opportunity to create the first ever anthology to highlight and honor our community at large. I'm proud to say he has become an integral part of our regular gathering and someone I consider a mentor and a friend.

The first four years have been amazing. I'm excited to see where the next forty-four years take us, and what we'll collectively bring to the table along the way. This book is dedicated to the potential of the blank page, the power of the open mic, and anyone who has ever found a home in either.
With love and gratitude.

— Jesse James Ziegler
Co-Founder, Creative Director and Host of Monday Night Poetry
City of Reno Poet Laureate (Jan '24-Dec '25)

Isis Atkins

10 Things to Do Before the World Ends

1.
Tell your friends you love them.
Don't let a moment go by without it spilling from your lips like a prayer.
Let the restaurant you share dinner at become your church at that moment.

2.
Write down everything you're too afraid to say out loud,
admit every love,
every mistake,
everything you wish to forget,
and remember.
Burn it in the ashes of the capitol building.

3.
Scream to the sky.
Yell "I FORGIVE YOU I FORGIVE YOU I FORGIVE YOU"
until you start to believe it,
until the words seem meaningless,
whichever comes first.

4.
Share an ice cream with your dog.
Let this be her last bit of sweetness while you sit
and watch everything around you crumble.
Promise to find her in the next life so you can love her longer.

5.
Grieve.
For the mess in your head you never got to figure out,
for the life you've always dreamt of but will never get to experience,
all the joy you'll never know the language of.

6.
Cry it all out.
Let it flood the Truckee,
drown the streets of midtown with salt water.

7.
Laugh as hard as you can.
Until they think you're crazy,
until you forget what's happening around you,
until the tears turn to belly aches full of joy.
Never forget this moment.

8.
Kiss a stranger,
or your best friend,
or your soulmate.
Fill the last little bit of time you have left, with love.

9.
Dance in the streets.
Sing and chant like your lungs
aren't covered in smoke and radiation,
like the news will finally listen,
like the politicians actually care.

10.
Rest.

Sammy Aucella

Porcelain and Prayer

They say
Time heals.
But no one warns you—
she's a butcher in silk.
No one explains
how she does it—
how Time is not gentle,
but a starving god
who feeds on what you love
before offering peace.

I didn't believe them.
Not when I was curled
on the bathroom floor,
wringing your name from my throat
like spoiled wine,
as if grief could be
bottled and corked.

Not when I buried
entire months
beneath bedsheets
and unsent confessions—
my hands, cracked maps
of everything I never said.

Time wasn't cruel.
Just a drunk
with bad aim—
bumping into memories
I'd tried to bury,
knocking over everything
with your face stamped across it
while I whispered,
Please—sober up.

At six months,
I kept your toothbrush.
At a year,
I still counted your name
in the seconds
between songs.

At four,
I stopped crying—
but flinched
when people said *always*,
like a spell
I was never meant to survive.

At seven,
I realized
I hadn't thought of you
in…well—
I don't remember exactly.

Which is funny,
since my days
used to howl
without you.

And when they finally did…
I didn't howl back.

Time didn't heal like a balm.
She healed like erosion—
slow, brutal,
dragging me through your memory
'til my skin bristled with bark.

Until every sharp edge
bled into something
strong enough
to hold me
and my silence learned syntax.

Time didn't steal your memory.
She threaded it
into the hem
of who I am now.
She taught me
how to carry you
without slicing
my palms open.

And now,
I think of that girl—
how she knelt before grief,
a throne built from your wreckage,
like she'd been born to beg.
How she screamed your name
into porcelain—
praying pain had a drain,
and mercy might flush you away.

I don't blame her.
I don't shame her.
I fucking bow to her.
I whisper,
You won't believe
who we get to become.
Not in spite of the fire—
but because of it.

Time heals,
But not like they promised.
She makes art from the ash,
hangs it in a gallery
your name beneath it—
and dares you
to stand there
and not weep.

Ms. AyeVee

Sticky Hands

Life drips with irony
like an ice cream cone too long in the Vegas heat
Excited anticipation
turned melted puddle on the street
I've never been very good at holding onto happiness
Felt it's comfort in the palm of my hands
as it slipped through my fingers
For a moment it's mine
a taste of goodness and joy
a gift I have waited too long for
a pretty little life with a cherry on top
but it was never really mine
Just another mirage in the desert
a trick of the eye
just another brokenhearted girl with sticky hands
staring at the ground
where a puddle of dreams once existed

Latreece Bass

Persistence

There is one word that describes the success to life. Persistence: it will penetrate the walls of failure like a knife. My friends, it will put wings on you and take you to a place that you never dreamed of—you will take what you have learned and what you know and rise above. What makes us queens and kings is battling a war that we won. Now that the war is over and we witness the risen sun. My father said only the strong will survive. Thank you, God, I feel alive, the skies are clear, and happiness is near. Nothing can tear me to pieces. This war that I've been through won't leave no traces and no scars on my face. Freedom I will embrace, these chains on my wrist have been broken, all my pain and sorrow has been taken. Those old dilemmas won't be missed. This ceremony is like a passionate kiss. Persistence is all I need. Persistence was planted as a seed. I have outgrown bitterness and sprout green leaves of kindness.

M. Colton Brodeur

The Atronach

My bones were woven by deft hands that spun the calcium
strings imitating the silkworm and bark spider.

My composer carved my teeth from moon rocks
she found upon the mountain tops that fell from the dark side.

Her plans for my flesh were to use fresh bark
from the hardest tree known as the lignum vitae,

but failing to find one at the nearest park, she settled
her mind on the rind of the mighty oak. My hair

she made bespoke from the feathers of a blue jay
that she asked for as a joke. After repairing the wing

that the mad flying thing—having flown into a window—
broke. My irises were strung together like peg and rubber

band art from the strands of sky visible only after thunder
clouds part. My heart, which is also blue, beats specifically

to the rhythm of her favorite tune, 'Dream a little dream.'
The gray matter of my brain was made by collecting

and mashing together a hundred things that aren't as they seem.
My hands she modeled after King Midas so that every soul

would turn gold at my touch, but souls like gold are so soft
for something so hard, so my Midas touch never meant much.

My vocal cords were forged by my father, modeled
to match his own, using the same piano wire he used to garrote

the last man to sit upon his throne. Several pieces of paper
were thrown into a hat to determine my gender.

On each piece was written something profane in a dead
language. They shook the cap and threw it in a blender.

My aspirations are the bottled-up dying breath
of several great poets who didn't live to see their worth.

My sense of humor comprised of everything ever said
to make my mother smile, which she had been collecting

from her own birth. My legs were built with neurodivergence
in mind, made to handle constant tip-toeing just fine, to run

wild but never win a race. My arms designed for physical labor
to push, pull, lift and grind, but crafted first and foremost

to embrace. I was constructed with the utmost care using
only the finest reagents my progenitors conceived of—and

while unbeknownst to them—I absorbed also their despair
I was made with by and for love.

Derrick C. Brown

Waltzing the Hurricane

Waterslide architects have been spying
the smooth of your back,

mapping blueprints
from the finger trails
adoring up your spine

stealing your design.

Do not keep asking me for more revelations, dear,
or I will just keep sending you to the back of the Bible.

Revelations 12:7.
And there was war in heaven.

It's still there.

In this light
I can see through your body.

Black Hills Indians wrapped your bones in arrows and feathers
for the day you make your exit, inspiring new battles in heaven.

Enemies sliced by the wit of your lipstick.

You are a Sunday porch I could do nothing on
and feel like everything was happening.

Let me pull my hurricane move—
a move to turn your gilded fortress to shrapnel—
to windscorch your overbooked rickshaws,
melting your slippers into glass formula.
Girling you out.
Bursting your leggings
into pink shredded wheat.

AAAAAAH!

Andromeda Carnivora
envy of novas
zing your flesh across twilight.

Stay asleep
so the aircraft aren't drawn to land
on the Christmas lights
crackling safety signals
from your eyes.

I saw you
panting in the oven of your skin.

Aren't you tired of awakening next to lost armies?
Sick of people looking for jade in your nostrils?

Subterranean teeth-gnashing orchestra.
Zebra killer.
Flexed duchess.
Carved cha-cha-cha.
Zirconia sass rock.

I want the theater without the drama.
I want the opera without the soap.

Lay in the stillness of a fighting-saints fairy tale.

Your partner is here,
a frog in a coma of kisses.
You, dressed as wonder,
screwed me backwards
with your
dyslexic kiss.

Fairytale saints fighting stillness.
Kisses of coma.
Here is partner your.
Wonder dressed you.
Backwards me screwed.
Kiss dyslexic.

Alon Burton

Shapeshifter

I watched you change just for a moment,
long enough to see your eyes gasping for air.
Your leather skin.
Teeth like razors.
You could no longer hold what was within.

A brand-new face just for the TV.
Claws on the wheel of your Mercedes Benz.
Armani suit on your way to the temple
to sacrifice a virgin to your bloodthirsty friends.

You won't let us leave this prison planet.
We are cattle for your army for snack or binge.
You harvest our fear for another dimension—
wormholes in the sea are what you're here to defend.

Hard to find a shape,
        shapeshifter.
Far from the right face,
        shapeshifter.
I saw you on tape,
        shapeshifter
You control our fate,
        shapeshift.

You won your fight with Ahura Mazda,
and brought Nibiru to a sudden end.
That cataclysm wasn't the end though—
restless 'till you see the Anunnaki dead.

You followed them into the garden.
Made them all hide in their pyramids.
You took their thrones then enslaved us.
Soon they're coming back, and your reign will fall.

Hard to find a shape,
shapeshifter.
Far from the right face,
shapeshifter.
I saw you on tape,
shapeshifter
You control our fate,
shapeshift.

Elisa Carlsen

Dear Mark Twain,

I am your Nevada Territory…queer, nostalgic and hammered to stone. A desert of riches extracted and abandoned, mid-way through.

Everywhere I look I see the ruins of time, the tailings, the dead towns, the beautiful ghosts who taught me to love something until it vanishes…and then to love it even more.

Many have come here like you, looking for gold. A metaphor so thoroughly stripped, even I won't touch it. Nothing grows where they have been.

This land is not for them. It's for the ones who give themselves up to be irradiated by the burnt neon glow of an atomic sun, whose light like mine, appears to disappear…just up ahead.

Scoot Carnahan

My Dog Has Nipples

There I was at the dog park.
"She's beautiful.
Or sorry, I should say handsome."
She looked at his penis.
Yeah. "Handsome."

I stared at her Starbucks cup.
Thoughts firing.
He or she.
The fuck difference is it to me?
My dog has nipples.
He has nipples and a penis.
His testicles were taken at 7 weeks old.
"Boy or girl" they ask—
I'm not sure how to respond.

Why does it matter?
Old women craning their necks to see my dog's tiny penis.
People apologizing at *misgendering* my wagging best friend.
Does the Border Collie Pit Bull mix care if he is called a *she*?
I couldn't care—
Oh, but people do.

Any gander of crotch they can manage,
Do they notice the nipples?
Did they see him squat to pee?
I don't think my dog knows what gender is.
He humps just about anything.
But so do girl dogs.
So why do you give a fuck?

I want to say,
He was born male,
but identifies as female.
Well, today he does,
it's in his strut—
that little spice in his,
Sorry, her step.

What will people think?
What is next in line?
Will they ask if my dog only humps girl dogs?
Does my dog go to church on Sunday?

"He's an American!"
A man said,
offering a small salute
to the dog that doesn't speak English.
Is my dog a nationalist?
I think that's unlikely—
Though dogs ARE pack animals.

I saw a bumper sticker
in a casino parking lot
"My dog is a Republican."

My dog is no Republican.
He doesn't have a job—
Always looking for handouts.
He hardly respects authority.
He doesn't sing along to Lee Greenwood's
'Proud to be an American'

He certainly isn't a fascist,
I wouldn't guess a racist.
He has a vote,
and I wouldn't let him go hungry.
I think he's a democratic socialist.

But maybe I'm just projecting, too.
Like they say, the dog becomes you.
So next time you look at my dog's tiny penis,
be a doll—Notice the nipples too,
And be sure to say thank you.

Savage Cute Bastard
For my dog, Mojave

Best friend.
Too simple a phrase.
Those amber eyes,
that orange brindle,
your white socks.
That strip of white running up your snout.
You savage, cute bastard.
I love you.

I'm sorry for being so mad when you tore my couch up.
I'm sorry for the moments you are home alone.
I'm sorry that I make you shake paw before every meal, before every treat.
But I want you to be a good boy.
You are a good boy.
The besti boi.
One helluva charming boy.
Thank you for coming into my life.
The sweet angel I needed,
you saved my life.
You savage, cute bastard.

I always dreamed of a dog named Mojave.
In that first moment I saw you,
I knew it was destiny.
You did too.
You ran right at me,
a little 7-week-old puppy.
We locked eyes.
We became a team in that moment.
You savage, cute bastard.
Soulmates?
Yes.
No living thing has ever made me happier.
Prouder.

Humbler.
More excited,
more scared.
More lucky to be alive.
You savage, cute bastard.

February 8th, 2025.
We got in my Jeep, I was nervous.
You crawled into my lap,
You crawled on my shoulder.
You fell asleep.
I cried the whole drive home.
I found my boy.
Sweet and beautiful.
Like spring in the desert you're named for.
And now, my eyes fill like a summer monsoon.
You're a teenager.
You're becoming a man.
I'm proud of us,
But I'm already missing the days of puppy,
when you fit inside my jean jacket.
You savage, cute bastard.

I'm a proud single dog dad.
Making it work on a wing and a prayer,
being my best
for my best friend.
I can't remember what it was like
before your morning cuddles.
Before the guts of stuffed animals were all over our den.
Before I had your wet kisses.
You mean the world to me—
you savage, cute bastard.

I wish I could keep staring at you,
scribbling my love in my pocket journal,
but I've got to feed you,
clean up after you,
pet you,

cry tears of joy for having you,
give you a treat and leave for work.
You're my world, kid,
I love you.
Even after you ate my plant,
ripped my couch,
destroyed my mattress topper,
wagging your tail like I should be proud.
You savage, cute bastard.

Handsome as the desert in golden light,
majestic as a warm desert night,
savage like desert flora and fauna,
like nature, you are perfect like a true work of art.
I'm honored to have you in my heart.
You savage, cute bastard.

Andrew Coffey

The House is Burning

I'm too deeply rooted in my faith
to know we can't always feel like this.
Mama said there would be days like this,
but it's been like this for way too long.
When do those days just become what it is.

Somewhere along the way we lost the plot.
The seeds we nurtured for all these years
were abandoned in the dark.

Things haven't been the same since the levees broke.
Things haven't been the same since Trayvon.
Things haven't been the same since 9/11.

Fly a plane into any sense of a future we saw for ourselves.
A knee on the back of neck for a country that's on life support.
Someone call in a school shooter with an assault rifle
to put us out of our misery

Our house is burning is fucking burning!
Let that good capitalistic growth keep them warm.

I would say ask for help but by the time I get to the end
of this the fire department and water
authority might already be defunded.

The little dignity we had left went up in flames.
Take a deep breath of that smoke
and you can smell us almost being great again.

A con man with a toupee and a cheap suit,
spoke about draining the swamp.
What about the snakes in the grass?
The ones that make it harder for the black
and brown people, LGBTQ, trans kids, and women.
The same snakes that wear a Klan mask with a MAGA hat.

They can't see the strength in our resilience

We are the monsters they made and I hope
they get nervous whenever they look under their beds.
Don't eat the rich, let their dead bodies decompose
and be a warning for all those that dare
to trespass next.

Shelby Contreras

CC and Cheap Wine

It's not that I believe or don't believe
in love.
It's not that I believe or don't believe
children.
It's not that I believe or don't believe
that I won't get to dance naked
on the beach in Greece.
My faith these days lies with people
that live on the streets, right off of Brinkby.
While I move into my house with granite
floors, yes, this suburban dream
comes complete.
Yes, you can stay with me.
Stay with me.

Camilla Downs

Tilt

a joyful baby birthed
defenseless
trusting
innocent
i pressed play
the game began
with a motherboard of pure authenticity
the controls locked from the beginning
i, a slot machine
the adults around me
feeding me coins
of love
of joyful times
feeding me coins of
hate
of conditional love
of praise for pleasing them
feeding me coins of
judgment
of unwanted attention
feeding me coins
that led to the betrayal of myself
feeding me coins
laced with
a culture of prejudice
sexism
misogyny
classism
stereotypes
colorism
white privilege
homophobia
transphobia

feeding me coins
until they hit the jackpot
of having me as they needed me to be
i traveled through life stuck on these default settings
society feeding me more of the same coins
i believing this to be the true me
nearing midlife the game tilted
the error reverberated
throughout my system
a crack was revealed
curiouser and curiouser
i poked the crack
the crack becoming a crevice
the crevice becoming a canyon
the canyon a decade long journey
revealing the code to unlock
character customization
customize I did
unlearning the bullshit I'd been fed
i collected new coins of
acceptance
solidarity
and freedom
devouring books, movies, articles and music
deleting the old codes
continuing to customize
and will continue to customize
until this Camilla game has ended
i reach high
grab a few stars
squeeze them between my lips
and swallow
the stars evidence
that showing myself grace
is the flavor they shed
i reach down
grab handfuls of grit
smearing it onto my skin like glaze
this, my shield against other's agenda

i am pieces of all my experiences
coded together
by the text of the books I've read,
by the poetry I devour
by the adventures I pursue
by the letters that form the words that make the sounds of
conversations
by the smell of coffee
by the salt water of the ocean
by the two kids I birthed and raised
by the relationships I've had
by the beat and lyrics of music
by the nectar of honeysuckle
if all of this is absurd
if life is simply a ridiculous illusion
i have no choice but to have fun
mostly anyway
i have no choice but to
continue customizing this character called Camilla
i have no choice but to
continue my conversations
with the moon and the trees
i have no choice but to acknowledge
i was at my most authentic on the day of my birth
and I will be again on the day of my death

Natalia Durán

Ella (She Is the Moon)

You remind me of the moon
in slivers,
everchanging
creating waves
ripples of change,
an enigmatic glow
coloring the night.
Your eyes
remind me of dusk,
a tint of darkness
in a pool of light.

The desert is loud
at night—
I thought I heard your voice
between fractured mountains.
In the heat of sage winds,
we walk
through the lamp-post-light roads.
My hair dries in curly waves
and your lips
plump from the heat.
You are in color blue,
holding my hand
as we stroll by.
All around us is big and grand,
the houses
the cars
the streets,
we pause by a creek;
in a garden of sunflowers
a single couch sits
dressed in plants and tools.

Home feels like that—
a garden of life
in our own living room;
your Italian art
and my old stereo
that used to only play blues.
At night we cook
we empty the bins,
take out the trash,
wash the plates.
We find rest in shared space.
How sacred it is
when home feels like that.
Home is knowing each other.

Erin Eddings

Jesus was… an Elephant… Never Forgets

How useless my bleeding heart has become,
how unnecessary is my played-out tongue,
when all I want to do is SCREAM
as these headlines relentlessly livestream
one
by
one
by
f-ing
one.

But no!
They don't come in singles.
More like eggs, they come in dozens…
Dirty, rotten, stinking dozens, these days
all my childhood friends are being swiftly, methodically
rather violently, dragged away—
PBS and
Public Radio
Public School
The Late Show?

Public Health.
Reproductive Rights.
60 Minutes.
Long-lost, restful nights.
The right to bear discontent.
The very NEED to know.
My neighbor…15…missing for over six weeks…
Who's next to go?

It's got me feeling paranoid.
The end of days…is it just a bunch of noise?

My Christian sisters be selling snake oils.
My Sisters of doubt be praying down doom.
Yet all the while I cannot…stop…staring
at this serene, almost glowing, elephant in the room
and she's winking — at me!
You see, she remembers one love, one tribe
She remembers being free…
      (I know you are…but what
      are…We…?)

She's the Trinity.
She's what you need her to be.
She represents!
She repartees!
All the nonsense, the shameless hate
we feel for one another,
feed to one another.
Breakfast lunch and chicken dinner winner.
One another.

It's clear as day and bright as night
while y'all trifle connection and sling misdirection.
This beautiful, Jesus-like mastodon
whispers sweet nothings in my tiny, human ears…
Be still
and know that I am
and you were always, in all ways,
here. Just here. Now. Present.
Peace. Love. No accident.
Let that heart bleed, sweet child—love is the new black.
You look so good in it—don't turn back.
We in this. One love. Remember.
We got this. One tribe. Re-member.

Steve Elegant

Mourning Breaths

Breathing in the pitch-black morning. Stale cigarette smoke from last night still hangs in the cresting light of dawn. That acrid taste in my mouth accentuates the bird song. There's life out there. There's barely a pulse in here. The rhythmic movement in the drapes emulates what should be my breath, but I'm scared to breathe in. It feels like a freezer in here. It's life underground. So much wasted potential down here. I can almost smell their sweat. The burning light of morning will come, and with it the coffee to bring a pleasant aroma to cover the unpleasantness. The unpleasant surprise. The wholehearted movement of another day. A cycle that cannot be avoided, even after you are gone. The intrinsic nature of life. Sustain sustenance. Shelter in shelters. Clothed in cloths. Breathe. The explicit acts that carry on existence. The value of fate accepted. One fate. Unavoidable to be voided. The stars spin brightly still. Steps on the porch. Strike a match. Inhale. Exhale. Let it out. There is more than this. There is less than this too. The weight of mannequins. There's light out there. There's light in here too. Move past the adolescent admonishments. Grab the door frame. Steady. Remember that you are meant for more than this. You are all meant for more than this. And it's time to wake up.

Fia Ewers

The Way in Which I Will Live

"Why give flowers if they will die?"

The reduction of my time on this planet,
the time in which I have been searching for the light.
I will hug the weight as I search synonyms for terminal diagnosis,
a guilty title given to blur the lines between
infinite and fleeting.

The weight of it, believing it is enough to hold, just as I held
a sister, a friend, a daughter, a poet, a lover.
Shape my heart with the ways in which I am human,
and my stubbornness will find a way to make more.
To speak beyond us, to levitate to a place between death
and life, and still choosing to hear the echoes.

I will melt into laughter with you amidst the war.
We can find the way to the sunlight and sleep in it.
I beg, let the light in.
Sprinklers kissing my ankles, winter's cold cracking
my bare skin, strawberries bleeding
juice in the core of paper towels.
A demand at a chance of imprint on this world.
I beg, let me do the same.

Find me in the place between love and loss.
I will lead you to the light.
I love you on purpose.

"Why give flowers if they will die?"

Everything has a pending fate.

"Why wouldn't I?"

Jean-Aléx Fonvil

WE

WE ARE THE BONES THAT ARE
STACKED ON TOP OF EACH OTHER
ONCE THE GRAVEYARD RUN OUT OF SPACE

WE ARE THE STEEL ROD ALL FORGOT DID THE JOB
BEFORE THE CONCRETE AND INSULATION
CAME AND TOOK OUR PLACE

WE ARE THE NECESSARY EVIL…
TO THE PEOPLE WHO NEED A SECONDARY EXAMPLE
OF WHAT IT MEANS TO BE GOOD
WE HAVE THE POWER OF POWERLESS, AND WEATHER CONTROL
WHETHER OR NOT WE ARE THE RAIN
WE ARE THE REASON YOU WEAR THE HOOD

WE ARE THE MESSAGE
WE ARE THE MOVEMENT
WE ARE THE METRIC
WE ARE IMPROVEMENT
WE ARE "THE CULTURE"
TO OTHER CULTURES

WE ARE THE TEACHERS
WE ARE THE STUDENTS

WE ARE THE LAMPSHADE TO THE ENLIGHTNED
AND THE ALARM CLOCK FOR THE WOKE

WE WERE THE FINAL FEATHERS
THAT FELL TO THE GROUND
ONCE WE WERE PLUCKED
FROM THE BACK OF HOPE

WE ARE THE GOD DAMN ROPE

THAT YOUR EARLIEST RELATIVES
GOT THE STRING OF LIFE FROM
WE ARE THE PAYMENT FOR YOUR ENTERTAINMENT
WE ARE THE NECK THAT YOU GOT YOUR GOD DAMN
ICE FROM
WE ARE THE EASIEST LESSON
YOU WILL EVER LEARN
AND THE HARDEST LESSON
WHEN WE ARE MARKED
"THE NICE ONE"

WE ARE EVERYWHERE.... YET

IT IS WHERE WE ARE NOT
THAT WE ARE FEARED THE MOST
WE ARE NEVER ALONE
WE ALL WALK SIDE-BY-SIDE
IN THE SAME STRIDE
WITH SAME GHOST
WE ARE THE RELUCTANT IMMIGRANT
OF AN UNPLANNED VOYAGE
WE ARE THE HOLLOWED HUSK
LEFT BY A SOUL SAVED
WE WILL NEED A SAVIOR
WHEN THE SAVIOR SAVES YA'
BECAUSE WE WERE OUT WITH THE PLANTS
WHEN ALL THE PLANS GOT MADE

WE ARE THE SHEPHERDS CHILDREN
WARE THE HERD UNHEARD

WE ARE THE LOUDEST CRY MET
WITH THE QUICKEST HUSH
WE ARE CONSTANTLY QUESTIONED
YET SELDOM MENTIONED
WE ARE THE EASE OF TENSION
AND THE ARENALINE RUSH

WE ARE THE OLDEST BLUEPRINT
FOR THE NEWEST SCHEME
WE ARE THE FOCAL POINT OF A FORGOTTEN DREAM
WE ARE THE ABSENCE OF COLOR IN EVERY SCENE
WHILE ALSO THE THING THAT MAKE WHITE LOOK
CLEAN

WE ARE THE PERFECTORS OF SILENCE
AND TALKING BACK
WE ARE THE RHYTM MAKERS
OUT OF WHIPS THAT CRACK
WE ARE THE OLDEST BONES IN THE GRAVEYARD

WE ARE BLACK
AND WE WILL
NEVER BE ASHAMED OF THAT!

Dominique Frida Francis

The Gospel According to Eve

In the beginning, there was sunlight
caressing her gold-brown skin, the feel
of the warm earth beneath her bare feet,
the animals and the flowers and the moon,
and with her the first man to discover
the weapon of knowledge, kept and withheld.

In the beginning, her hair pooled around her
as she swam in clear waters, her breasts
joyous weights breaking the surface tension—
uncovered, unvilified,
mountains unconquered, unclimbed.
Her hands gathered fruit, she tasted
their sweet goodness never imagining
its juice could cause such hardship
or that love could be so cruel.

In the beginning, her body belonged to her alone
and there were no thoughts of owing life
to an unborn stranger, allowing it to rip its way
into a world echoing with her screams,
or undying loyalty, a homecooked meal
to a man who claimed he gave her a name
she knew in her bones from birth.

In the beginning, his eyes traced
her movements through the garden,
he kept silent vigil as she approached a doom
he alone had been cautioned against.
His devil's deal with a similarly jealous god
led to their banishment from her garden,
but at least he got to watch her cry out in agony
as she bore the weight of his child,
got to subjugate her for the crime of being
woman and beautiful and free.

In the beginning, a woman wore
her hair unbound, savored the weight
of her lovely bare breasts, basked in the sun,
tasted the fruit produced by the
fertile offerings of a new green world,
watched the stars above her move
with eyes un-lowered in shame,
felt in her bones her worth as a woman,
and was punished for such sins.

Elisa Garcia

Gold Hoops

My mother had my ears pierced
as soon as someone with a piercing gun could shoot me.
I've been called *chillona* since my adornment.

Hoops originated in Mesopotamia, Nubia, and Egypt—
since ancient times,
they've been a way people show up to the world.

Some days I have a hard time showing up in the world.
I carry grief for all the love I have lost.
Sometimes it's hard for me to speak.
Especially when people don't see me.

Sometimes being Latina, I feel like a song I was never taught to sing.
So disconnected.
Shut out of my own history.

As a Latina,
my hoops are my strength.
I swear, I put on red lips and gold hoops,
and I am fucking invincible.

These hoops give me power.
These hoops are a shield.
Have you ever met a poet
who was actually confident?
Bitch, with these hoops I am unstoppable.

Growing up,
I often heard the term "Ankle holders"—
slang for oversized gold hoops.
Some people connect them
to a woman's supposed promiscuity.

So—
Call me radical.
Call me free love.
I will dance with desire.
Continue to be unapologetic.
I refuse to be quiet.
I will take up space and I will not shrink.

The Garcia Girls

The Garcia Girls are part Valley Girl part *Mi Vida Loca*.
My sisters were my first best friends.
Shared secrets and made pinky promises regularly,
tolerated me since I came out the womb too soon.

Have been there for every awkward moment—
have loved me, through braces and a bowl cut and a mullet.
When I lied to my mom about shaving my legs
and said razor bumps were heat rash.

Every heartbreak—
when Robyn told me she could not love someone so much younger.
Broke my heart through Myspace messages.
When the first boy I loved married our best friend.

Every cringey moment—
when I told Victoria I lost my virginity
in the backseat of a church boy's BMW,
belly laughed and told her friends.
I stained the interior to match the paint job.

The Garcia Girls taught me how to love myself
before I could even find things to hate.
Told me that my chubby was cute,
my brown skin was nothing to be ashamed of—
taught me how to embrace myself.

Victoria showed me how to tease my hair,
how to rock gold hoops,
and to ask for forgiveness,
to get back up after falling from grace.
How to ask for help - which I still need to work on at times.

Rita showed me what it's like to have love for everyone.
How to apply too much eyeliner.

She also taught me how to shotgun a beer.
I taught her how to speak her truth even if it hurt,
that I could be her safe place even if she was scared
to share her story.

Regina showed me what I do not want to become.
Demonstrated compulsive behavior, bloodshot eyes,
and disregard for others.
Taught me how to be stubborn and in turn taught me
how to be a fighter.
I do not mean this as an insult, but a lesson.

The Garcia Girls are the beginning
of a blonde, brunette, and a redhead joke.
We've all got tattoos despite our parents' wishes.
Some form of anxiety or depression,
the same wide nose and dark brown eyes.

We shout *I love you, bitch!*
when we head out the front door
or greet you at the family dinner.
We are not *chismosas pero*, like
we are always ready to spill the tea.

Victoria, Rita, Regina -
My sisters,
my teachers,
my best friends.

Anna Glenn

The Miracle Is Already Here

Now, it's just about what we do with it.
The miracle already happened. Nothing became something.
The world came to be. We exist and we know it.
We exist and we get to BE with each other.
It does not matter what you do now. You ARE.
The entirety of our lives is just playing with this miracle.
How much fun can we have?
How sweet can we be to each other?
How well can we pay attention?
To better listen, to better see the miracle of it all?
It is not an easy answer, but it is not dire either.
One step at a time.
One experiment at a time.
The world is my lover. The world is rich.
My life is rich simply with my paying attention.
I do not need money. I need my soul. I refuse to sell it.
Maybe I've already sold it, but I'm stealing it back.
They had no right to it in the first place.
How dare the soulless offer money for our souls?
It's not my problem. I'm just trying to pay attention.
No accusations, just honest observations.
I'm good at this. I am good at the things that matter.
It is not hard. It's just so easy to forget, to get lost,
to stop breathing deeply. I will remember to smell the roses.
I will plant them. I will send them my love from miles away
and I choose to believe that they receive it.
We choose what we believe and in that we are Worldmakers.
We are Gods. It's lovely enough to make you cry.
You should cry about it once in a while.
Maybe every morning. Maybe every meal.
Maybe every goodbye. I've had enough goodbyes.
I am sure that I will endure more. I do not need
the strength for it now. I'm not sure endurance is strength.

I'm not sure endurance is a choice.
The same way nakedness is not a choice.
We're just born that way. And quickly they try to fix it.
It's just not safe. But it is inevitable. Our nakedness
is inevitable. Our endurance is inevitable.
Inevitably, someone will try to fix it.
I won't let them. I will hold the baby naked to my chest
and I will endure, and I will not let them take the magic away.
The miracle is already here.
Heaven is already here. Let's not ruin it. Let's not ruin
the stars. You used to see more stars in the sky.
Is it worth it to stay up writing, reading, working,
if it means fewer stars? Something in me says no.
I think that something is God.
When God speaks, let her.
When God speaks, Listen.
It is not difficult to know what is right.
It's just that the world has been so long forgotten,
so long lost. How do we get back to where we are?
How do we get back to where we have been the whole time?
How do we get back to the miracle that is already here?
I ate breakfast this morning.
Maybe we just have to keep eating breakfast,
keep holding the naked baby, keep holding each other.
The answers will come thousands of years ago.
The era will end yesterday. The lover has already said
goodbye. I'm trying to convey the impossibility of it all.
I'm trying to extend the invitation.
That's all I don't even know how to do.
I don't really know anything. I'm just trying to pay attention.
I'm just trying to speak the language with no words.
Imagine my words are kisses. Imagine my words are the wind.
Imagine something, DAMMIT!
It's alright because we can still imagine.
It's alright because we are still here.
Not all of us.
There were infinite goodbyes tomorrow.
Broke our hearts into infinite pieces.
Infinite stars.

They will shine as brightly, one day.
They were here, one day.
My breaking heart and all the stars in the sky.
How can you choose?
It is an impossible choice.
One of the impossible choices we make every day.
It's okay if you don't feel the miracle.
I feel it enough for both of us today.
Tomorrow, I may need your help.

Mackensi Green

Ghost Hunting

      The bedroom door with air as hands, swinging
open then closed. Swinging until the cat pushed
      through the door. All the usual noise from the backyard
becomes singular. I don't need to check to know
      the red eyes are outside the window again. I call
for you and call again. I don't get up, even
      with my bladder brimming, not even when the hour
passes and the house is done tormenting me. Here,
      with your bedspread and a king, I make myself
smaller. Lose myself in the crack between mattress
      and headboard. My first encounter with ghosts,
I can't help but think we have better stories.
      Like when you called the police on your own shadow,
do you remember? Thought someone was in the house
      and even though I saw my shade next to yours, heads
smaller, I let you call anyway. I wanted to see
      what kind of man, the one who drove up the driveway
with the headlights off, would come and decide this moment,
      or my life, was not an emergency.

Rachel Grey

I Carry Home

I don't know exactly when I came back
home to myself but maybe
I found a piece of it
when I stopped having sex
that made me feel far away from myself.
Maybe I picked up another little piece
when I let myself question if silencing my inner
compass and suppressing my muse
was worth being accepted.
I carry home in my body, now,
because I learned somewhere in my twenties that I'd never feel
peace while I abused and starved myself.
Maybe I found a way back to myself in every therapy
appointment,
where I learned that I could survive misunderstandings and
disappointments,
where I learned that I could break open and withstand the weight
of the truth.
I have always been after the truth.
I am hungry for it now—insatiable for life and all its complexities.
I carry home in my body,
and I'm making up lost time for
the years spent trying to numb, dissociate, disappear.
Now I guzzle down experiences,
now I try to see how much goodness I can take;
how much honesty I can give myself.
I carry home in my body, the pieces
are a beautiful mosaic of all the people who've held me
while I cried
and of all the people who showed me what safety feels like.
I have always had a profound softness in me.
I carry home in my body.

Nikki Leialohalani Herschend

A Lion, a Saber, and a Crown

"They erased us from the textbook,
but my blood remembers,
even when the world forgets."

My grandmothers didn't whisper,
they warned.
I am the story that colonial tongues choke on.

I don't need a crown,
I am the blood that made one.
I was not made in your image,
I was carved from conquest.
I am not your myth,
I am the correction.

My name—a blade that cuts.

My great-grandfather
broke nations like bones,
left kings shivering in their palaces,

Their gold swinging in his fist.
Nader Shah of the Afshar Dynasty,
crowned in Iron.
Sword of Iran.
Storm of the East.

And I?
I come from the storm.
My blood burned Delhi
before the US and Israel even existed.

I carry kingdoms in my marrow
and war in my mouth.
You want my rhythm,
not my revolution.

I am not first-generation.
I am every generation
that refused to burn.
I am the child of war drums,
of calligraphy and carnage,
of turquoise domes and bone.

I am from the fault line—
from a place where blood overlaps
I am the border that speaks back.

I carry in my veins
queens veiled in indigo,
the generals with rust in their teeth,
the poets whose tongues were daggers.
I was raised by women who sang
while the world collapsed.

And yes—
I am Iranian.
I am Turkish.
I am Azeri.
I was born from Tehran's breath
and Azerbaijan's bones.
A border child.
A lineage that could not be simplified.

I remember
the oil lamps in the hallways,
the copper bowls of pomegranate seeds,

The women humming ancient hymns
as they ground saffron into the skin of rice.
I remember
how my father gave me a name
that could never be Americanized.

I am the heir of heat.
The daughter of dust.
The storm that bows to no nation.

When the war drum sounds,
you will look for allegiance.
But I was forged
before your sides were drawn.

Your country wants my voice,
but not my volume.
Wants my beauty,
but not my bones.
I am not your immigrant dream.
I am the nightmare of erasure undone.
I am throne and torch.
I am not asking.

I am naming.
I am claiming.

Do you feel it?
This weight in my voice?
That's every ancestor
you tried to forget.

Jahangiri.
Beglarbeigi.
Translates to
king of kings
world conqueror
you will speak them clean.
You will speak them whole.

My name is a saber,
A lion,
a spell,
a warning.

You want my story
in palatable portions.

But I will not serve myself sliced.

I am exile turned eruption.
Call me a refugee—
but know
I'm the reason borders crack.

My name does not need to be shortened.
Your tongue needs to stretch.

So, prepare,
because I'm coming with
all my ghosts,
all my gods,
all my grief.

Daughter of War.
Keeper of Ghosts.
Lion from both sides of the blade.

If you fear what I carry,
it's because you know what you buried.

Priya Hutner

Unspoken

Aspen leaves flutter.
Cragged peaks loom.
The last rays of light slip behind the crest.
The high pitch whistle of a lone osprey.
Darkening skies outline the shore.
Gentle currents ripple across the shadowy water.
A lone head bobs.

Venus rises.
Slowly other celestial bodies join her.
Plunged into the darkness.

The acknowledgment of time shatters the night.
A tear slips.

The months have taken their toll.
Mumbled, slurring, hacking, fits of laughter.
Thinning, graying, worsening.
Like a snake shedding his skin,
writhing to escape from its form.
Tick Tock Tick Tock.

Wasting away,
like a hungry ghost unable to swallow.
Trapped in his own glass cage,
thrashing.

Words stuck in his throat.
He fights to swallow.
He fights to survive.
3-6 years.
Tick Tock Tick Tock.

I fly east.
It will be the last time.
Time to say goodbye.
Time to heal old wounds.
Time to let go.
The past dissipates in the light of death.
Old pains, an elusive shadow
pales in the face of impermanence.

Some let go and surrender into the unknown with ease.
Some fight a valiant fight.
Some fear the uncertainty of the impending transition.
Are we ever ready to leave this plane of existence?
Are we ever ready to tread into the abyss of unknowing?
Will our loved ones, long gone, be waiting to greet us with open arms?
Or do we dissipate into the fabric of consciousness.

Wheels touch down on the tarmac.
Palm trees sway.
The air is thick.
Sweat drips between my breasts
A pair Sandhill Cranes shriek a deep throated cry as they fly by.
Flipflops slap on asphalt.

The door to the lanai screeches.
We embrace.
I ease onto the couch next to him.
He points and stutters.
Read it, I ask?
He nods.

I take the book from his hand.
He closes his eyes.
I clear my throat and read the dog-eared passage.
Death, Time, Oneness, Love—
each sentence dropping him deeper into his reality.

In a room without a voice.
Pages rustle.
He writes in his journal.
He pushes it toward me.
A treatise of love from father to daughter.

He points at me,
passes the journal and a pen.
I write.
I forgive.
I let go.
We sit in silence for a long time.
"It's ok to go now," I say.
He scribbles quickly and pushes the pad back:
"I am afraid."

I tell him it will be ok.
But I don't really know.
A tear drops onto the lined pages of his notebook blurring the ink.

One last hug.
One last cry.
One last I love you.

It's a somber journey home.
Raw and unmoored.
Death arrives soon after.
Not without rousing him out
of his morphine-induced state one last time.
And then it is done.

I feel him in random moments.
The old New Mexican dish on my counter,
a crystal on my altar,
a carved eagle on the shelf,
black beans.
We move on.
We live our lives.

The yellow haze of the full moon rising.
Reaching through the pines to meet the billowing gray.
Clouds skirt across the sky.
In the stillness of her reflection,
a lone bat flies.

In the quiet of the night,
I breathe in.
Thousands of stars dance above me.

Sophia Jacobson

Her Masterpiece

With her hands
she cross-stitched generations
even after the arthritis kicked in
every stitch giving way
to another eye color
that looks like my sister's
brother's
nephew's
niece's
and mother's
as her hands got stiffer
She continued to suffer
pushing the needle
into the fabric
of our DNA
and pulling it straight
to ensure a lack
of unraveling
But as her joints
continued to harden
so did her worldly ambitions
She may have knotted her tails
weaved in her ends
and yet my seams
have come undone
For her heart is
holding Heaven's gun
any moment now
Her hands will slow down
She will no longer be able
to continue
this embroidered
familial tree

and thus the
needles,
hoop,
and thread
that make up
Our tapestry

will have to be passed down
to her genetic memories
but I do not know
who could carry
the weight of the thread
She schlepped so gracefully
through the joint pain
Finger pricks
tremors
and delicate familial politics
that thread has been weaved
into every Bostonian request
for a cup of coffee
and books about murder mysteries
and ice cream late in the evenings
and fresh picked berries
laid out on a tray to freeze
for summer pancake mornings
and every last Marion memory
She
is the creator
of all of us
being
She is "my grandmother"
to the person
who loves her
more than anything

Levi Johnson

Like an Occultist

Dear Diary,
I talked to a man over coffee about my destiny.
He told me there were thousands like me,
and I could achieve the life of my dreams.
It was then that I knew.
Satan needed me.

Dear Diary,
It's my first day;
I hope the other cult members like me.
When I arrived at the compound,
it didn't look like much,
but Cult Master Dave was very welcoming.
After his doomsday allocution,
I was awestruck and eager,
to spread Satan's boon far and wide,
perhaps—one day,
I could be a Cult Master too.

Dear Diary,
I think I'm getting the hang of this.
In the morning I have laundry duty,
you see, at first it sucked,
the stains are unbelievable,
because we sacrifice a lot.
Something about "culling a flock", I don't know.
Perplexed by the stains,
that's how I learned,
all is possible through the power of Satan and Oxiclean.

Dear Diary,
Great news,
I've been chosen for something important.
Six months ago, I wouldn't have been chosen for anything.
I'm told it's big.
Maybe it's time for my destiny to come true.

Dear Diary,
Ignore that this is written in blood.
It's all I have in this cell.
Apparently my "big destiny" is to help
summon a demon named Azrael,
and by help I mean I'm supposed to be sacrificed—
free up my human shell for this entity of hell.
I'm pretty bummed because this means I'll miss Taco Tuesday.
If anybody finds and reads this,
much to my chagrin,
please heed this warning:
never, I repeat, never,
join a cult,
when you're a virgin.

Samantha Jones

Am I Porn Yet?

I was lookin' at porn the other day,
   I do on rare occasions,
See what the trans girlies are up to,
   Broadcasts from distant stations.
One post caught my eye though,
   Not 'cause of titillation,
The title felt like the answer
   To some great unsolved equation.
"Am I porn yet?" she asked,
   (I'm only paraphrasin')
The question rang so clear and true
   It demanded explanation.

You see, there's two ways to be a tranny,
   The first inspires lust,
The second way, unfortunately,
   Inspires true disgust.
You might think me a bigot,
   Leaving my sisters in the dust,
But here's the secret, honestly,
   They think both of all of us.
We try and try to be the tranny,
   That makes all the men bust,
But once they have, their shame sets in,
   Sometimes they murder us.

No, what I want is to live free,
   Not coveted, despised,
I want these men to see us for
   The light behind our eyes.
I'm beautiful, creative, smart,
   Though often unwise,

And thankfully a lesbian,
   I can't imagine *dating* these guys.
What's worse is they're in power,
   Publicly they treat us like flies,
But behind closed doors they're jerkin' it
   To the women they despise.

Trevor Owen Jones

Luck and Its Torments

"The mind is brushed by sparrow wings,"
specter and superstition surprise us yet again,
we arrive at the start of the ouroboros on course
of its dining, divining
seashells from sandmatter,
materialism merits the psyche
and warehouse new yokes to shoulder.

If you give away a knife, you give away your luck.
Dropping a big spoon means a major fool will visit you.
Seeing a poor duck in a dream: you must soon begin a tremendous task.
If someone closes a knife you opened, you will be unlucky.
A rooster crowing at night is an ill omen indeed.
Bringing eggs in after dark (bad luck).
Prevent nightmare by letting the toes of your shoes face east.
If you wipe your glasses with a dollar bill, they'll never steam again.
If a tea kettle boils dry, a storm is coming.
Sleep on a crumb of wedding cake, your dream will come true.
Dreaming of ascending a ladder? Trouble.
If you dream a gray horse, you will receive a letter in the mail.
Frogs croaking during the day? Rain.
Lucky is he who walks in the rain.
If you hit your funny bone, two women will visit.
Spider at noon? Good news.
Sneeze before breakfast? Tears before dinner.

Look into a mirror ringed by a wreath: now you're blind.

Britt Keehn

A History of Displacement

My aunt turns on the light at 5 AM
when my eyes are adjusting.
"Rise and shine!" She nearly shouts as I wince.
She is undeterred
comfortable
bustling around me like an ant,
moving around a blade of grass
fallen
on its path.
She's undeterred
comfortable
in this house that has been her home
for nearly as long as my life, and I think,
if I found such a home today,
I would never know it as long as she has known this home.
If I married the right one today, I would never know a 50-year
marriage.
My home is a busted plastic-handled teaspoon, a few mementos of
a dead dog,
a disintegrating toy bear,
a phone that I am blessed to keep ringing,
and the people I am blessed with who pick up the other end.
I am
too many years for bad luck.
I am habit of uninhabitable
lack of habitat.
I adapt
stability floats further away,
a dot on my horizon.
I have lived too many lives to be one thing
made of too many pieces
born of too many zip codes.
I stay in

homes that are cluttered
with lifetimes.
Shelves of memories,
drawers of belongings,
an intricate unspoken organizational language spoken
only by those who live here
where I am visitor.
I am alien.
I am clutter
taking up their space.
I clutter.
I am welcome, but
when am I leaving?
I am welcome, but
they have plans.
What are my plans?
I am welcome, but
not home,
nomadic by necessity,
migratory by means of habit.
I tow clutter,
I nest in windstorms.
A favorite pillow,
a Ziplock of perfumes,
a longing to be undeterred
comfortable
home
someday.

Courtney Kelly

The Ginko

is so ancient a tree
that the entire class of insect,
which once pollinated its blossoms
has gone extinct;
so too have gone the creatures
which once ate its fruit.

That is not a poem.
but there is poetry in it:
in the way that I am still
writing you poetry
though neither the actions which caused my affections to blossom
nor the creature who once ate of your fruit
survive
I release my words to the wind
like pollen
they scatter and land
upon others of my kind
who, having lost both the propagator
and the reason for propagation,
have continued,
in defiance,
to live.

The Ginko has been used for thousands
of years as a remedy—
a treatment for failing memory and blood disorders.
Though modern science would say
that there is no proof of
its efficacy.

That is not a poem.
But my god, isn't it the same
with broken-hearted poetry.

Cratered When We Kiss

Salt-slick goddess, you
burned up meteor-like
in the atmosphere above
the 405. I spun-out
four wheels, five lanes, black
tar stripes; my windshield
fractaled on impact.

Calamity.

Jane. Darling. You
were iron-spine-stomping,
sulfur-spewing, nickel-pinching
mercury. You made me mad as a hatter.
I was phosphorous glow
when we kissed, cratered earth
when we kissed.

Look at the mess
you have made of me. The bay
where there once was land.
The mass extinction.

Brandon Leake

Dear Daniel

I used to be a teacher.
I had the distinct privilege
of attempting to turn a classroom
of academically narcoleptic youth
into a thriving village,
where their dreams became their pursuit.
And though I was their teacher,
I feel like I was the one learning the daily lessons.
For instance, I had a kid named Daniel in my class—
one of the oddest students I'd ever met.
He had the potential to be anything,
and of all the things in the world,
he decided to be
a knucklehead.
So concerned with securing digits,
I figured instead of thumbing his nose
why not give him some pointers
about how putting himself in the middle of her business
could be offensive.
So, I told him you gotta learn the rules of engagement.
Made him pinky promise he wouldn't do it again,
and I come back the next day to a face palm—
seeing him trying to spit game once more.
I loved that kid.
I wonder how he's doing, now, during this pandemic.
See, most folks would never relate to the agonizing fate
that laid in wait the moment he walked outside those gates.
Half his teachers were only ever concerned that he was late,
not realizing a house ain't a home for everyone.
He would tell me:
Yo, Mr. B,
You like the older brother I never had.
For him...

family is a subjective thing.
For those he shares a bloodline
tore holes opening his bloodlines.
His wounds were numerous,
but not as populous as the excuses
he'll make while around the general populous.
And now I'm here caught in cerebral gridlock
about a conversation we had.
He asked:
Mr. B do you believe in heaven?
I told him I do:
Yeah, me too.
Shoot sometimes I wish I was there instead of here,
'cause dying can't be harder than this,
but at least 2 hours of my day is cool.
Bell Rings
Aite Mr. B I'll see you after school.
He told me that my classroom was his safe haven,
how here he found
chosen kin in scholastic companionship.
The way friends turn to family
when you've assessed your address ain't what's best...for you,
but now that schools out he's once again orphaned
to a home he's not sure he'll make it out of.
And this is what it's like to live on the razors edge of today,
playing Russian roulette with your tomorrow,
not caring if you survive
or make the headlines of the noose.
In America suicide is the 10th leading cause of death,
and particularly 18% of teenagers reported they have considered it.
So, 1/5 of high school-aged youth
have said the world would be better off,
if they never saw they own reflection again.
Now Brandon why bring that up?
Because in the face of a virus that has caused the world
to slam to a screeching halt,
I know Daniels mind is still racing,
contemplating whether or not it's worth trying to survive this distance.
How isolation has caused him an anxiety ridden existence.

But it's not just him
There are youth all over the world,
trapped within the asylum of their minds
with no hope of release.
Children caught captive in houses
where their souls are worn down against the heat of concrete,
and everyone says it the asphalt.
Yet we could be the difference.
But even with these devices in our hands,
we can't bother to extend one.
Daniel I'm so sorry for the ways I've failed you.
I pray I'm not too late in my realization that
we have been created for the sake of community.
Our unity is the only way we survive this.
Please don't let the journey end here.
You have fought too long. Take a pen and a pad
and turn your pain into purpose, for you are worth it.
You are worth every breath, our day, hour, minute, second.
This world is better due to your presence.
Daniel…You are far more than some knucklehead kid in my class.
You are the kin I've adopted into my heart.
Here you will always have residency.
So, don't leave because I couldn't bear the vacancy.
So, please Daniel choose life
And come home!

Anthony Lomando

Nassir

On the opposite end of the Earth, there's a town
with a palette of colors, entirely brown,
and it goes by the name of Gardez.
It's a city where buildings are built from the dust
as, to thrive in that place, it is something they must;
or at least, that's what everyone says.

In a high mountain desert where summers are hot,
though the meters of snow in the winter are not
what I thought to expect what I went.
When I landed in August, the tarmac conducted
it's shimmering heat through my bones, unobstructed;
unwelcome in weight and ascent.

See I'd come with the Infantry, fighting cartels,
though they worked underground which is all just as well
as our presence was something to fear.
I remember a day when I hit the bazaar
and I stopped at a shop where a man with a scar
said "Hello there, my name is Nassir."

And his English was perfect, as he used to be
an interpreting linguist, one not unlike me;
in an instant, my interest was piqued.
He said "Visit my shop and you won't need the others.
Let's sit and have tea as we're basically brothers."
I sat with him three times a week.

He would haggle with merchants to lower my fees
and he traveled to Kabul whenever I needed
since I wasn't able to go.
And one day when I went to my resident vendor,
he said with a smile, "Hello there my friend,
there is something I think you should know."

See, the Taliban told all the merchants whenever
they'd send us their famous exploding love letters
as we were their objects of lust.
So on days when the locals had gone into hiding,
the rockets were coming to preface the fighting
and so we prepared as we must.

But the problem with knowing of incoming bombs
is at some point they'll notice you're acting too calmly
so all of the stakes must be raised.
I remember the day when they gave the bazaar
and the hospital building a view of the stars
and the peddlers and patients a daze.

It is known that the Afghans are not fond of pets
and Nassir gave me warnings I never did get
which is fair, with the many I've raised.
But my soldiers would feed all the dogs and the cats
which was good for morale and relief from the rats
and it seemed like it worked for the strays.

I remember a day when the nomads were mortared
and scent of their cauterized flesh was recorded
forever inside of my nose.
As it turns out, their hounds are much cuter by day
and their vicious consumption kept Afghans away
though it helped the buffet decompose.

It was after that point that I took to his lessons;
especially cultural factors of essence
like rules of reciprocal gifts.
When you do for another, the culture compels
them to do unto you as a way to dispel
any debts that have come to exist.

I promoted his service with soldiers around
so his commerce was prosperous, patrons abounded
and I hadn't known my effect.
But he often did favors so helpful to me,
though delivered with semblance of some subtlety;
it was rare they were ones I'd expect.

When he noticed me tired from overnight missions
and brought me a drink to improve my cognition
by way of surprise nicotine.
We would sit and interpret the news on TV
and there once was some opium laced in my tea
as a gift, though a gift unforeseen.
But the biggest most valuable favors of all
were the ones, undelivered, I often recall
as the Taliban wanted his head
With his family in danger, I wasn't allowed
to go help, nor asylum and visa, endow,
and there's nothing more final than death.

He gave us his all, though we never committed;
with years of assistance and help, unrequited,
they left me forever in debt.
I still speak with his ghost when I'm watching the news
and he's one of from several that I get to choose
as I haven't let go of them yet.

Aimee Lowenstern

Poet's Envy

I want to write a poem
so, I reach rummage inside me,
find you and yew and unicycles.

Hard to draw a drop of blood
that has not already been used in metaphor.

Hard to look at the moon unenraged
by my own lull in lunar
language. The moon is a unicycle
already taken, perhaps

by a unicorn. A unicorn
that dips their horn in nightink
like the shiniest best pen nib,
writing with their head down,

writing on ship sails as they cycle
over the sea, spokes of moonbeam
turning turning, and they are never afraid
of a misspelling or a frumpy adjective,

and all their punctuations rhyme with
constellations, their commas shooting stars,
and their eyelashes are so long and pretty

which I know
because one drifted down upon my heart,
toppling me from my tricycle
and bruising my rib—

They pasted a glorious apology letter
upon my hospital window,

and I, pulling splinters of teardrop
from my wound, knew
that not one word of their masterful mope
was a sign of caring for me.

John Merryfield

The Shining Path (El Sendero Luninoso)

How do you say sea in Quechua?
Si.
And with this question I am alone
in my mind
and punch drunk by
moonbeams
twenty
miles from my destination,
or maybe right here is home.
It is an impossible night of paddling.
There is a dark sea
and a light
totem of the
Milky Way,
the small bright stars
swirl and sink around the sides of my paddle.
Before leaving the
house, her note
of encouragement read:
the white bougainvillea
blossoms are marking
your path back to the sea,
follow them.
I have only one rule:
to cause no harm.

Eric Morago

When They Told You It Was Them and Not You (But Really It Was You)

Quit while you're ahead.
Don't ask them to coffee and play the what-if game—

>*What if I called less?*
>*What if I called more?*
>*What if I didn't call them by the wrong name in bed?*

Stop. You could build a funeral pyre out of unnecessary questions.
Put that torch you carry down. Listen.

I know there is a pressure building in your bones—
an earthquake tucked behind your ribcage.
How your skin is a blues ballad, its notes scribed in braille.
How your gut is a knife fight.

But the truth will not set you free.
Wings will not grow from the blades of your shoulders
if you learn the reasons why.
Knowing will make an anvil out of you.

They are not a monster for unloving you—

but if it helps, take the clenched fist of your heart
and extend its middle finger out for the world to see.
It is okay to get angry. Let loose the tremor.
If you must, let others trace their hands over your flesh,
let them learn the sad songs stretched over your body.
And whenever you are ready, sheath the knives.

I will be here all the while, reminding you how to suffer
for love
without doing anything too foolish.

As for those reasons—
those little gremlins creeping around the words
it's not you…

they are merely gears in the machine of a universe
turning about, without us having to understand.
A gorgeous complexity of physics, designed to run on its own,
regardless of our having learned every pattern and principle.

And even with the occasional black hole, there is still so much light.
There is still so much glow in you
that it travels millions of years into the past

where ancient civilizations build temples in your name.

Do not forget to pay tribute to yourself.

You are lightning striking the same place a thousand times.
You are the tree that is struck, which does not burn.
You are scorched earth, but never ash.

Lies I Tell My Therapist

Everything's okay. I don't try to dodge
my childhood like an oncoming bullet
train or play a game of chicken against
it. I get along with my parents just fine.
There's nothing complicated about our
relationship. We are sky and sun, moon,
and sun (never mind the sun is a giant
volatile ball of gas). Growing up was easy;
my mother never took too many pills, never
fell down the stairs. My folks didn't divorce
only to remarry each other my senior year
of high school. And my first girlfriend
never found my parent's lube shoved deep
into the couch cushions and accused me
of wanting to try "butt stuff." My brother
didn't go homeless and addicted for years,
and my father certainly did not let him.
My brother never spun a revolver's barrel
loaded with five rounds of someone else's
prescription drugs or tiny Ziplock baggies
packed with the wings he thought he needed
to find God. It's okay, okay? When he died,
I wasn't angry—forgave our father faster
than a shotgun blast. I don't open my skin
as if my body were guitar and my flesh,
strings to be plucked. I don't keep a favorite
razor blade, tucked between the pages of
my Grandfather's Torah he left me after
he smoked himself to death. I know there's
an afterlife—believe in all the good things
that wait for us there. I don't dream of dying,
veering off the side of some road. Or dream
of not studying for a test, or being on stage,
having never attended rehearsal. Or falling.
Or nudity. Or falling while nude. Anxiety?

I don't have anxiety. I dream all the good
things I know I am—that you tell me I am.
I do the work, exercise gratitude like learning
a new language to someplace I cannot afford
to visit just yet, because I am definitely not
still in debt. I don't owe anyone this shame
I hoard under my mattress. I've never cheated
on myself with guillotine lovers, haven't lost
my head to the woosh of terrible decisions.
I absolutely do not toss back more whiskey
than I should, every night, like I'm practicing
a sword swallowing act for a sold-out crowd
of exit signs. Really, I'm okay. I'm okay. I'm—

Pan Pantoja

Transmission

This is for those who stacked
bodies to reach their fathers
and told stories of giants
and making love to star people
in desert heat.
Who begat babies of
unspeakable wealth.
Who harvest yet more metal flowers
from the scorched earth.
Who arrived here from Martian soil
to force logic
down the thoughts
of the Athenian princess.
Whose Kundalini moment
Awaits us still.

Who created babies
capable of loving all
the creatures of this world,
producing strange fruit and
seeds of abominable Greek nature.
Who rule and are ruled in spinning top fashion
taking turns in this futile roulette.
Who created communicative devices
to replace what is natural connection
and abilities the rational mind
simply cannot comprehend.
Who bend spoons and
spout fortunes for sideshow acts
for skeptic skeletons
and energy vampires
awaiting a savior or a second coming.
Well I been cumming all over this world
since puberty failed to suck the magic outta my heart.

I say to all you wayward way seekers,
all you back yard soap box speakers,
you forward peace thinkers
gonna mastablast you out your sneakers.
I say you are he who sets us free
and you are she who saves all humanity
and we are the people old seers said
would come to bring into flower minded fields
and blooming heart chakras.
Beautiful sun spots dancing with the moon
knowing full well we can never really touch her.
Resting in the earth breathing in her bountiful bosom bliss.

Reshaping creation
imagination manifested fully
walking ancestral dynasties into the present
and there is no time like now!
Undress your spirit
stroll naked down your city streets
or small town courtyards
proclaiming shouting with the voices
of a thousand seraphim angles:

I know the truth.
Wealth is not measured in belongings or bonds or gold
and I know the truth.
You are infinitely larger than your bodies.
Endless is your soul.
And I know the truth.
Power is laughing at those who seek to control
and I know the truth.
You are not alone you are so not alone
and I know the truth.
There is more going on than my eyes can see.
Yes I know the truth
and it has set me free.

Griffin Peralta

Live Ammunition

In the bottom of my closet
There is an old wooden chest stenciled
with the logo of the US army and the words:
LIVE AMMUNITION.
When I was a teenager, I bought it on the side of the freeway
from a man selling military
surplus out of the back of his pale blue 1974 Ford F150.
I blacked out the word "AMMUNITION"
So it just says LIVE now.
And for years... it was the box I only opened
when I needed the reminder.
LIVE
It demanded when opened.
LIVE!
It reminded when closed.
And inside... I kept everything I ever owned worth living for.
In polite conversation,
I call it a memory chest, but this is a poem,
so here I will call it a life vest—
It's full of things that save lives,
like gas masks,
like bullet proof vests,
like
the post card my father sent me from the last place
he ever tried to commit suicide.
It says:
I'M SO SORRY
to this day, it is still the only time he has ever apologized to me.
Beneath that there is a caricature painting of my grandmother,
On the back of it she wrote:
Boy...
Don't let the bastards get you down.
And I won't,

because right next to the portrait is a box cutter,
It hasn't held a razor in years,
Not since I took it from my first best friend,
broke it. It's just a plastic brick now,
It can never hurt anyone again.
Other oddities inside the box include
the pair of panties I stole on the night I lost
my virginity, the flashlight I shone on my face
when I told my siblings ghost stories
and the second-place trophy I won at a speech
competition in 2006—
the one that made me feel like these words
were worth something... and so was the
speaker,
But the finest thing in the box is an empty cigarette case.
It belonged to my mother once.
Tucked inside, carefully lettered in my very best
5th grade cursive is a note that says:
I love you, Mom.
You can do it.
She carried it for years,
told me once that it finally helped her quit...
And when she picked me up from the county lock up
for the last time, she returned it to me
with a note that said:
I did...
So can you.

Melanie Perish

Apparition at the Edge of the World

Hawks cry. The penned dog barks.
Breath breaks the bud of silence,
and the murmur of leather on stone
echoes my ordinary sorrow.

Yesterday's small cruelties
are forgiven under weedy clouds
that crest and fold like river waves.

Last night, a long-ago lover died.
When I finally slept, a dissonant apparition
with her face reminded me
I sleep on the edge of the world
where sooner or later everyone falls off.

She and I were feral cats, the ones
left by summer people who thought pets
were seasonal like bathing suits. We swam
in the clamorous dark, carnival calliope
and bare-bulbed lights in the distance.

When she asked me to move away with her
I asked her to stay with me.

Now, I walk as though I swim this hour—
sink as a wave knocks me under. I surface,
take that first breath,
the one that lets you know you won't drown.

Atticus Pizzo

Rally Cry

Camera phones do for us what the news won't.

The revolution still won't be televised.

But it's being archived by street cammers and cataloged
on private hard drives.

History is being sequestered away for a later date.
A time when acknowledging the full scope of the story
won't be dangerous enough to get yourself vanished by those who
hate.

I saw this one Instagram post, where two friends are archiving
the history of trans folks.

They're taking open submissions for files to squirrel away and
keep safe.

An endeavor we'll thank them for, years from now,
when we are tasked with the job of re-educating children
whose parents had their legacies taken away.

It might take generations to level the plane.

Fascism has been a plague since anyone can remember.
The great library of Alexandria was burned to the ground
to keep the future of humanity oppressed.
The history of queer people tossed into fire pits
every century or so at a dictator's behest.
The holocaust is being scrubbed from the internet as we speak.
The voices of Palestinians are being bombed in droves
to keep their oral history from being heard
and we all have a front row seat.

The future is holding its breath.

That means there's a good chance it's gonna turn blue.

Blue, like, clean oceans.
Blue, like, open sky horizons.
Blue like butterfly bushes on hillsides with the resurgence
of bugs under rocks and fireflies in the night.
Blue, like the kind of democracy I'd like to see.
Blue like flying Pride flags freely.

We are on the precipice of capitalism imploding.

I know this because we're always a dollar short
of the changes we want to make.

Our economic systems have become unsustainable in this way.

Wealth has been amassed in bank accounts of tech industry
tycoons
and without economic power, the people's freedoms
are too easily taken away.

We are so skint for money that change has become
a dissonant idea that we can't save up to pay.

Some years ago, I told myself that we're two shakes away
from a modern Renaissance movement.

The artists, and storytellers, oral history keepers,
are all used to being broke and in the margins.

We have carved out a life here.

We know how to make ends meet outside of society's reach.

We know that survival means passing around between us
our meager excess in order to keep our friends on their feet.

Nothing pulls the spirit of humanity out of the darkness
quite like the starving artist.
The new Renaissance is a place of history made real
through the compression of life's harshness.

It's an unstoppable virus. When we amass a trove of our stories
and keep them safe and close to where our heart is.
They will be there to unveil when facism is vanquished
again into the tarpits.

This is the success I see in the strength of Indigenous family trees.
It's contained in their strong tradition of oral histories.
Histories and truths kept between lips,
instead of vulnerable on paper that slips...
between fingers and crumbles to ashes...
when a dictator dictates that their knowledge is too passionate,
too powerful to be kept alive,
so colonizers hand out blankets with pox laced in the threads
and call it goodwill for cleanlier times,
off with their heads.

If you find yourself a dollar short,
One paycheck away from being homeless,
One sick day away from losing your job,
One moment away from losing your sanity and you feel all alone.

Fall back into the arms of art.
Fall back into the teachings of those who came before.
Find a way to tell a story that can't be burned.
Take all your paintings, and stories, and hole them up in storage.
Find a place to keep them safe through the storm.

But most of all remember to fall.
Fall into rooms like this one.
Give your energy to those fighting the good fight
 who will hold you in arms.
And take their story on your lips and carry it to the next room.
This is how we keep the chain of history unbroken
and unerased from the archives on tech farms.

The Renaissance is imminent.
We're on the precipice and the time is nigh.
When we march in the streets and hold our signs high,
we are unstoppable like the pressing of a tide.

And in time we'll come to find,
After all the ashes of our burned histories rise,
The knowledge we've managed to keep
will come tumbling back down from the skies.

The ocean will be made blue again on our exhale.

The future will stop peering from between scared fingers
and recover from shame.

We will see eye to eye without having to poke
out the eye of those who reign.

We will overcome this culture where an eye for an eye
is dragging us swiftly into the reality of Gilead and pain.

In my heart I know that if we keep our oral histories safe,
Those who picketed on the right side of history will rise
again, and crash through the gates.
Keep the faith, what we as artists
and keepers of the storytelling tradition carry,
is our most prized means for escape.

Dani Putney

Explorers of Darkness

Our 12-year-old necks craned forward,
my Nintendo DS backlit & humming
from the tabletop, I botched my valediction.

I'm destined to disappear.[1]† I couldn't
tell you then what it all meant,
tears scouring my cheeks to reveal

bedrock only grasped in retrospect.
You didn't understand, but how could
anyone? *Thank you for everything.*

Temporality is funny that way.
Your freckled knees, the fiery springsnails
inching down your legs—a yesterday

I cannot lose because the timeline
was never tangible. I simply remember
fingers doused in blue light, a screen

narrating our dissolution. *I'll never
forget you.* I try to conjure your face now,
full imago, but I no longer have *Mystery*

Dungeon to guide me. You were my first
fantasy, evangelical impossibility
as it was, always grabbing my wrist

on the soccer field & grazing my hand
on the couch. *You have to be strong
on your own.* I miss this most

---

1 † Sentences presented in italics come from character dialogue that appears during the ending scene in *Pokémon Mystery Dungeon: Explorers of Darkness* (also *Explorers of Time* & *Explorers of Sky*).

from our alternate universe, two kids
unafraid to touch, any *more* a question
refusing to answer itself. We were,

weren't we? & I cried because I knew,
didn't I? Pikachu to Mudkip, me to you.
(The light is getting brighter.) On the verge

of 13, our *us*, that roguelike crevice
in spacetime, would soon vanish,
replaced with gender, body, flesh.

It must have felt right—dark room
somewhere in between, handheld
console as candle—to say farewell here,

cool hardwood underneath our feet.
I'm sorry. I think I finally get it, J.
I'm so lucky . . . you were my friend.

List of Suitors

Please review the preapproved catalog
of eligible bachelors for the client.
Rank the individuals from "1" to "6,"
with "1" being the best fit. This information
will help to improve our matchmaking
algorithm. Thank you for your time
& cooperation.

Δ

    ___ Gentleman 1 breaks up with me
because I correct him on the use
of the word "amiable." *We'll never
be equals. I don't have a Ph.D.
in anything.* Será.

    ___ Gentleman 2 kisses me with monster
tongue in front of the gender-neutral
bathroom. It's *Saltburn* night & our bodies,
ablaze. But he's looking for "friends"
& doesn't want to commit. *I'm just
too busy. 57 is a hectic age.* Será.

    ___ Gentlemen 3 & 4 are lawyers
from out of state. I fuck one, then rush up
the hotel elevator for the night's
encore. The second man sucks
the lube off my dick & doesn't falter.
We kiss & I taste a recursion. *Why
would anybody let you go?* Será.

    ___ Gentleman 5 wants to take a bath
together before the evening's romp.
I need you to hold me. I have no Lush
supplies, so we stoop in tepid tub water.
I've fantasized about this moment

with you. Later, I hang his lasso
on my wall & wear his Cattleman
to the rodeo. Será.

___ Gentleman 6 tells me he's *truly
versatile*, my pleasure *important* to him.
He fucks me spread-eagle & I learn that
bigger things aren't always better.

Him finished: *I absolutely hate bottoming.*
I don't expect a flip—maybe we'll switch
next time—but I still have to ask to be
touched. I ghost him but rematerialize
when desperate. Será.

Δ

Please submit your completed rankings
to the email address listed at the top
of the catalog—no hard copies will be
accepted. Our firm appreciates your effort,
& as a token of our thanks, we will send you
a $15 Starbucks gift card upon receipt
of your email. Have a wonderful day.

Pax Robinson

Find Another Way

Thunder shook the Earth
like a frustrated lover,
jagged, unbalanced electricity lit up the sky,
sizzling all around.

Then nature's Slurpee machine rained down
balls of ice collecting in our backyard
like eager crowds on a big game day.

I held your thigh while the thunder rolled
and you quietly let me.
Its softness helped to dampen
those all-around hard primal sounds.

Our cat was under the bed
waiting with the dust bunnies
for more peaceful times.

Then it stopped
and the trees sighed
and the crowds started to melt.

You could feel the silence walking up the street
like a guest you've been waiting for—
putting fresh sheets on the bed
clean towels in the bathroom,
but just as they're about to softly knock,
the sirens start
their wailing sounds. Surround us,
each one a small pocket of disaster.
Someone's own thundering and lightening.

I wonder what got bent and what got smashed.

Whose particular lives came completely undone in a flash
of light from the sky that scientists can explain
but our dumb human hearts
are just as ancient as they ever were.
Back when Zeus was hurling lightning bolts
down on our heads,
when all of us were hiding together
under Earth's unmade bed,
we didn't know why our most powerful god
was mad again.

But we could speculate
and tell each other stories of jealousy and rage
understanding and hope.

That's what happens when people are alone
together in the dark,
trying to remind each other
and themselves
that the sun will rise again
and out from under our beds we will come,
the ones in our hearts and the ones in our heads
and we'll see the mud and mayhem,
the trees that fell and the ones that stood
and I hope we will remember what lightning bolts
have the power to do—
a force stronger than Zeus and science
to bring us together.

First in the darkness and then into the light,
to remind us of our scared kitten-hearts and brave thighs,
to remind us that the stories we tell
can help us through the night,
that the morning sun is far
from the only source of light.

Jason Sarna

First Day

You are handed a black plastic bag
that contains the tanned skin of an animal
you never heard of.

The skin is cold to the touch
and smells like wet dog.

You reach inside and pull the skin
out of the bag like a rabbit out of a hat
but this rabbit has no   body.

Ta-da!

You drop the skin on a makeshift table
made up of two sawhorses
and a sheet of plywood
covered in razor blades
spools of black fishing line
and a variety of needles.

There are also blue latex gloves.

A big baldheaded dude with tattoos
known as Employee B shows you the ropes
and you get to work opening the eyelids
and thinning the nose
and the lips
with your trusty razor blade.

From there you cut the ear
just above the lower lobe
and remove the cartilage.

Every so often another employee
grabs the skin you are working on
and places it on an animal-shaped mannikin
like a coat.

This is called a test fit.

Once satisfied
the employee returns the skin to the table
and you continue to razor the eyes, lips, nose and ears.

Next you sew any holes from bullets
or otherwise
with a needle and fishing line
until the tip of the needle jams into your finger
and you draw blood
and Employee B shows you how some super glue
can heal that shit right up.

Power drills and cordless sawzalls
echo throughout the shop
as music plays in all directions
    90's hip hop
                    meets mariachi
                                    meets classic rock
meets your head wants to explode
from all the noise.

This is what you signed up for after getting fired
from your cushy real estate job
because you have problems falling in line
and submitting to authority.

You were making 21 but now you're back down
to 15 dollars an hour in the year 2019
where the rent is $1950 a month
and you have a master's degree in the fine arts
and over 65k in student debt
because you wanted to become a writer
and thought school was the way
to make that happen.

But no one wants your novel
about the lives of Regulars and Artists
and you're living with a girlfriend for the first time
which is cool and all
but you question if she loves you
and you can't stop thinking about smoking DMT
and re-entering the realms in hopes of understanding
the secrets of the universe
and why your friend
who had the same name as you
and introduced you to psychedelics in grad school
took his life back in Idaho
like Hemingway
with a shotgun to the head
which was a fantasy that used to bring you great relief in your 20's
but after your friend pulled the trigger
you now know that you can never kill yourself
so you do what you do to live on this planet and survive.

All in all   it's not so bad.

It's like being in an art class
with a bunch of real mother fuckers
doing real mother fucking shit.

Much better than being in an office
with a bunch of fake mother fuckers
doing fake mother fucking shit.

Actually…

it's a bit more complicated than that
and saying one thing is fake while another thing is real
is your anger talking because you still feel hurt
over being fired.

Cheer up!

You always said you wanted to be an artist.

Here's your chance.

God, Family, Country

These three words mean everything
to the hunters I interact with on a daily basis
yet these three words mean nothing to me.

I suppose I understand
(now more than ever)
how God, family and country
can mean so much to so many
but the reality I inhabit   at this moment   in my life
is a reality where God, family and country are dead
and no longer exist.

There was a time when God, family and country did exist
but even then it was hard for me to give a shit
about three words created by man to give man meaning
in a meaningless world.

I partly blame country music and churches and politics
and all the families who live in complete and utter dysfunction
but claim to love one another
for making me the way that I am.

I say we abandon God, family and country
and return to a more natural state.

The dinosaurs lived quite well without God, family and country.

That is   until the asteroid hit.

I'd much rather be taken out
by a giant rock from outer space
than killed in some war
while serving my God and my country so my family
who doesn't even know who I am
because I don't know who I am
can have a better life.

Everything seems backwards
with these three words:
it's like you have to say a bunch of prayers
have a bunch of kids
fly to Africa
and kill a zebra, giraffe or lion
to fully understand
what any of these three words
mean these days.

I don't have the time or money for any of that.

If I did
I doubt I'd spend it on some bullshit
you can easily find at home
while sitting on the couch with your eyes closed.

If sitting around isn't your thing
you can put your shoes on and go to the mall.

There   you can find God, family and country
and whatever else you desire.

Chris Warren Smith

Walk to Eternity

I walk my path patiently
with one instruction
to pay close attention.
So, I honor that by
smelling the flowers
along the way to divinity.
I'm in no hurry on
my soul's journey
as a thought of
avoiding pain
pulls me back,
a thought of
pursuing pleasure
pushes me forward.
So, I keep walking.
Depression slows me down,
anger speeds me up,
fear stops me in my tracks,
but I keep walking.
Distraction steers me left,
revelation keeps me right
as I keep walking
faithfully
towards home
where my
beloved awaits
to hear all about
my adventure
to return to myself.
One…step…at a time.

Raymond Solorzano

What is Burning Man?

Burning Man is located at Black Rock City, but it is not what you think it is. This is the first thing you see in so many ways. It's slow to take a hold of you, weaves a steady stream of tolerance through the pathways of your mind. It will test your patience, your strength... it exposes you. It will push you to personal tests... and forces you to let go a moment later. Then reminds you of so many things that matter; you just may not know if that's just a haunting memory that is a lie - but you will find out soon.

It's a city of lights, mayhem, art, personal expression, love, death, pain, poetry, music, with a dash of a wonderful roller coaster ride that may scare the shit out of you. It's a beach with no water that will drown you quickly if you stop paying attention for two minutes, and it has no lifeguard on duty. It will drag the stories out of you that you don't want to tell, and you likely don't even know exist. Tells you if you listen, who your friends are, but will likely scream at you who is not.

It tells you that you should have hope... but suggests "hope" is a lie parents tell their children, so they won't be afraid. It is not what you think "it is," yet somehow it is exactly what it is supposed to be; and that is her secret (shhhhh). BUT... you need to come with no expectations, that is your key you need to keep hung around your neck to unlock its doors.

It is Mecca, but it is not an art festival, it's not a religion, and it's a place that provides you no peace and quiet. It does not let you get away but tries so hard to toss you out on your ass for no reason at all; at least not for a reason you may recognize just yet... but just give it time. Makes you look hard at the mirror of life, and perhaps you may see a reflection of yourself there.

The city tells you not to be a Sparkle Pony... but tells you to be whoever you are in the same breath. Teaches you radical acceptance and attempts to show you not to secretly judge. It is your mom & dad... just don't look too closely. It reminds you of the horrible time of your life and will try and take advantage of this. It props you higher than you expected to be. Gives you a different view of the world. It helps you build a family and points out to you why you still want to have one; for some.

The city will judge you without prejudice, she has her own set of hidden rules. The playa takes you to where it wants you to be. She makes you wander and interrupts your plans every chance she gets. She is not a woman, not much of a man. The City is set down in the middle of nowhere, and Mother Nature wants no trace of her. And the City has it all in one little magical place, and She will punish you harshly for considering this.

So why do we come?

It's a place to say your final goodbyes and get those long-lost dusty hugs. There is so much unseen beauty... and you will be amazed, but don't blink or you'll fall into the kaleidoscope, and you will surely get lost. You will so hate Burning Man in so many wonderful ways.

You know you want to come, but I assure you it will be better next year. Don't come, come, the City does not give a shit, but there may be a few that do. You can speak their names with a dusty smile only one time of the year. And if you're lucky you have a vial of playa hanging upon your neck so you can smile again out of the blue someday soon. And oh, that dust, penetrating every orifice of you, you will certainly love that too.

So come, don't come, the City does not give a shit, but there may be a few that do.

Because culture jamming... it's all the rage, and all the cool kids still do it. And I will quietly laugh that you took so much energy that caused you to question life, while asking yourself why you even come for this abuse. But you know why, and you will want to come again next year. Because the story does not exactly repeat itself, and…It was always better next year. And of course (as I smile), you'll be better prepared next year.

The only question you need to ask yourself is, "Am I a night or day burner?" Answer is to be both and, "Fuck your burn."

Baylee Moon Spear

I Am a Doll

I was born a man
but that cage didn't fit me.

The masculinity prison was so encroaching on my happiness
I searched for the key.
I dug it out of the place where it was buried deep inside of me,
and freed myself from the patriarchal system that benefited me.
I let go of the male privilege and respect
I accepted that my standing in society would change.
All so that I could live as the woman who I'd always been.

You see transphobic men hate me,
because I looked at the cage and fought my way out,
and now I'm dancing in the sunshine
while they are trapped in their narrow-minded boxes.

I became one with the Devine feminine
 that was deep, deep down where no one could see.
I changed my name keeping my initials, because B names suited me.
Just not the masculine one that my parents branded on me.

B A Y L E E

This arrangement of letters frees me.
It's the name that fits my whole being.
My middle name is Moon—the astral force
in constant transformation she controls the water
who is always reaching up to greet her.
The doll in the sky who watches us at night.

Spear is the last name of my mother.
I cut off my dad's Holub like necrosing flesh.
Baylee Moon Spear. My name in its totality.

I am a doll—
in that I built my womanhood from the ground up.
It wasn't given to me.
This place at the table was fought for.
And I still have a terf or two say that my seat
is not a valid seat.
That their version of feminism doesn't include me,
but if your version of feminism depends
on what reproductive organs I possess,
you're no better than a conservative man
who just sees women as objects for breeding.

Your narrow-minded version of womanhood
leaves out so many women—
it's astounding not just the dolls.

The women whose genitals vary
from the textbook definition your obsessed with.
The women with mastectomy's.
The women who can't have children.
The women who've had hysterectomy's.
The intersex women whose chromosomes
and reproductive organs vary.

I am a doll.

You see I take hormones that help my body
match the version of the woman that my brain
wants to see.
But these hormones weren't built for me.
They were built for cis women experiencing
hormonal imbalances or change.

If these women take hormones are they less of a woman?
Or is it just me?

I am a doll.

People think I'm playing dress up.
They think I'm just wearing the clothes,
doing my nails, wearing makeup, changing
my pronouns, name, updating governmental documents,
waiting on waitlists, dealing
with transphobia, almost being killed
three separate times, loosing friends and family, being
discriminated against at work, having the government
become my number one opponent,
have laws tell me where I can pee,
having laws try and challenge my very existence
and having to fight with insurance companies
all to play pretend.

But aren't we all just playing pretend?

I mean gender is quite literally societal expectations
that we are spoon fed at birth
by our elders who have it in their brains
that this gender performance must go on.

You see we are all trapped inside this cursed auditorium,
playing our parts in the gender charade—
but us friends of Dorthy have broken out.

There was a secret door that was sealed shut—
give a lesbian a power tool and anything can be done.

We are sitting in a meadow outside eating a picnic.
Come join us—*that* show *was* exhausting.
It's ok, the dolls don't bite—
the furries might, but only with your consent.

Come enjoy the sunshine.
Aren't you glad to be free.

I am a doll,

and I'm so proud to be.
I love my whole existence.
I wouldn't choose to be cis—
I love my version of womanhood.
I wouldn't change a thing.
Doll am I.
Doll is me.

I am a doll.

Don't you dare call me a he.

P.S.
Eat your heart out JK Rowling.

Larissa Storm

Van Gogh

I love sunflowers—
How they stand together,
Turning toward a light
I see, and feel,
But I hush that it doesn't always
Reach

Tall and bright
Like they were made
To belong to one another
And I watch them,
Apart from them,
I touch their petals,
And feel the oils
Sticky
From where light reached them

I love them anyway

And dandelions--
I wait for them to go soft,
For the wind to loosen them
I wish on every one.
Every single one.

I find that I care enough
To want,
To hope,
To blow something loose
And maybe it will,
Find a place to land

We all need wishes

Even, the moon--
What it's like to give away it's blue
To wait to become full again
After being cast in shadow,
Silent and hungry
For that light

Afraid to name it lonely
With all its rovers,
Tides,
Its watchers
Writing poems from far away

I admire that noble satellite
I do not wish to be it
As romantic as it is
To be brave
And alone
I do not want to haunt the skies

I love sunflowers, and I need to wish

Cheyenne Scott Taylor

In Your Room, God Is Easy

So, we were there together, with everything blossoming
& twisting black & blue,

& I swore I saw Jesus

hanging all around your room

& he was so in love with us, I could tell,
because it was the most obvious crush I've ever witnessed,
I mean really, I was almost embarrassed for him.

He moaned & groaned endlessly about how your empty walls
were to him like some soft eternity stretched
across a wooden canvas all set up & birthed
just for his smallest of children to paint on
in their own strange mix of watercolor explosions—

all just for his wildest mistakes to fuck up
with the circles they have trained themselves to run in,

but I also know what goes up must inevitably come down.

So, what I suggest is that we drop the fucker for now,
tell him we'll get back to him later, because it's ok,
I'm sure the guy is used to it, & he will forgive us anyways,
won't he?

Because we can always get back to things later,
& this is important to underst &,
that it is because nothing is actually waiting on you
that you yourself can wait & wait & wait,

but to jump off from all of this, to take a leap of faith here,
I want to talk about how

you said it's cute that I try to believe in god

& how you talked about how easy that would be,
how the answers would all be there, & nothing would be strange
& unkempt & restless, &

how it would ultimately be too easy for me anyways.

I could only agree, with all of it,

because what I really know for sure is
that if this is who you are in the pale light,

& you know this to be true, so you better do
something about it.

You better have the guts to look at who's stabbing
you right in their eyes, right in the back of their eyes,
'cause that's where we all really live anyways,
we live back & back & back & back there,
we hibernate under & over ourselves,

& this is something everyone's parents should tell them,
& maybe they did & maybe they didn't,

but I know I need to hear it
so, I'm here & I'm telling you the same thing now
& I want you to know
that there is nothing harmless about living.

There is no right path.
There is no harmony.
There is no certain way to spend the day.
There is no easy breath out to be had when the clock strikes 12.
There is no big one calling you home for dinner,
& in this same vein

there is nothing harmless about the whole thing.

It's full of cutting & scratching & searing skin
from bone & chopping the fat from muscle,
& so there is nothing harmless about my feet moving
deftly around the earth in however manner I tell them to,
or about my heart suckling on my own tears,
or about your brain beating against your skull.

There is nothing sweet about it, any of it,

but then there is nothing evil there either.

& you need to know this, you need to feel it,
that it's just something that must lay itself out upon you,

that it has to crawl up your back & you have to flail
around like a degenerate & you have to beg for mercy
& then you have to let it lay you down for the night
& let it tell you how you belong to it
& then you have to cry out:
*no, no I don't, I belong to myself & windchimes
& sourdough & poetry.*

& sincethis is all necessity, since we are under fire
& we are the snipers atop the hill,
& we are the gaps of air in our own life support,
& you know this & I know you know this,
but it's got to be said out loud,

We now need to talk about how

we move & we push &

we slide & we drift.

But quickly, soon enough, there is stillness
coming up as an undercurrent,

& so then I know thatit was always stillness,
really, even then, see, because even when I was afraid,

I was still in a sunny place in your library reading *Pale Fire*,

& all of me was loose & hanging onto glimpses
of nothing, of nothing at all

& so the way I see it is that we've got four good h&s.

Four good feet, four good legs,
four good shoulders, four good eyes,
four good ears.

So, we ought to hang Jesus from your ceiling,
 have a conversation with the guy,

because, I mean, what other way do you want to spend tonight?
Is there any better way?

I've got my whole life for this,
& I don't have a home to get back to now anyways,

soI think we ought to taste Jesus' blood
& think about papayas & about how all my shoes
are too big for me & about how you cannot forget
how your father said you haven't changed since you were 11
& you can't tell if you agree or not
& about how my father will die an empty silent man
& that is why I am loud
& try to swallow the world up whole even though I know
it might just be intent on swallowing me.

But even so, we ought to let life bleed us dry,
don't you think?

So in this way, we can hang from it
& grasp at straws all night long like they're monkey bars
& we can laugh about how we will never get it right
& then we can feel the weightlessness
of our own bodies in this mess. We can whisper to ourselves:

Please move, just move, somewhere, anywhere.

Karen A. Terrey

Three-Legged Horses

You're going to have great education, much better than it is now, at half the cost.

— The president on his cleaving of student services from the Department of Education in preparation for eliminating the department.
(*New York Times* March 21, 2025)

Let's say you own all the horses
a stable of them, velvet muzzles reaching
over stall doors to lip your open hand.

You want them to win the race,
to run as fast - and here, a newborn foal,
four legs splayed like a stool to brace

against each other, wet bits of straw,
a child's collage, stuck to nostrils.
Let's say your horses raise their noses, whinny

into wild wind this equinox of Spring.
Their metaled hooves clatterdance
around the sparrows pecking grain.

Look, it's better not to look - for now.
People tell you the purse has changed,
don't you know? People ask you why

don't you streamline - your sleek horses
aren't winning every race, by the way,
these runners you've built through years of test,

experiment. Some step back, some forward,
for sure. Some flounder, find small injuries
slow them down. Trainers sleep in stalls

for little pay. Others deliver hay and oats.
Saddles, bridles, bits and shoes.
Maybe honey. You aren't winning all the time,

and money, too. Help us out.
We sent the expert. Already, in your stable.
To see where the problems are, to see

how the horses - well, now you see
it hasn't been working.
They've cut off one

leg from each to see where the problem
is, to help them run faster. Now
we will see what isn't working,

and in just one day we saved all
the money. Not the foal.

Em Tomeo

A Dog Still Loves You After You Beat It

No
No, the dog is confused
The dog knows that you are home
Safety
Warmth
And because of that it loves you
And when all the good things go away
All the dog knows is to be hit
And the dog learns to growl
The dog learns to bite
The dog can't choose that path
It is marked by the first night

A person still loves you, though
A person knows there was never home
Or safety
Or warmth
And they chose to love
They chose to create when there was none

The dog didn't choose to love you
So the dog cannot choose to stay

And we people are so stubborn
That once we create it
Once we choose it
We have to stick to it
Like our lives depend upon it
It becomes our night and day

Even if my life depends on
Leaving in the dust
How to say goodbye
To something you built

A kicked dog winces
Because it thinks it will be kicked again
A kicked person
Teaches themselves to like it

TWOSHAE

Exclamation

a.) sudden strong emotion

no pain in my chest
im not anxious
the butterflies have left
im calm and collected!
like standing outside
looking at the moon
but all i see is you!
the sky is clear
no rain, no clouds
no noise that's loud!
this love is quiet
love isn't violent
love is still there
even when it's silent!
your eyes shimmer
like milk chocolate
melting in summer!
i want to spend my
days waking up next to
you with your leg
intertwined with mine!

i'll love you past the
grave, forever!
ill love you past death
past our bones and
our flesh, forever!
forever, together, love!

Logan Veith

More Than I Can Carry

Life is long
I've gathered much along the way
More than I can carry

First I carried my life in a backpack
All I needed, I could go anywhere
A book of poetry, a joint, a dollar
A bottle of water, a knife, a pen
I'd use it all up, then fill it again
Soon, it began to burst at the seams
It couldn't hold the weight of my worries
Nor the heights of my hopes and dreams

So I started carrying it all in a car
And I could still go almost anywhere
A pad to sleep on, a tent, some shoes
A pillow to dream on, a wallet, some booze
A gallon of gas, a journal and pen
I'd use it all up and refill it again
But soon the car couldn't tow the weight
For one heart is heavy, but two is a load
And it's many hundred miles to my desired fate

So I went and got myself an apartment
It held the load, though now harder to move
A television screen, and a couch for two
A job to hold down, and a promise to you
Then came the immovable steadfast home
To hold all the things that weigh us down

I still dream of running free
With only a backpack to take with me
But I've gathered more than I can carry
And when it's too much
You say, don't carry it all
Just carry your love
And we'll share that load together

Iain Watson

Black & Blue

The weight of 1500 yesterdays
weigh heavy on our soul
it's not always the skin
that the burdens bruise
but the walls
that these sanctuaries hold

We've housed an army
of a thousand regrets
wrapped them up in prayer
found God in our own reflection
only to be blinded by the glare

The devils don't play fair
illusionists playing the role of savior
the greatest trick they ever played
was to turn us against our own neighbors

They find ways to break-beat the spirit
till it bleeds out blues
so we seek the melodies
deep within our trunks
needles to weathered grooves

Singing hymns of the broken
to upheave up a revival
baptize ourselves in vibration
and script out our own bible

We dance in different tongues
flicker flame between breath
translate every syllable to love
and celebrate the details of death

Each poem a headstone
to a memory we had to bury
becoming the authors
of these graveyards
that our bookshelves carry
I'm only the bearer of stories
the seeker of truth
the dreamer of tomorrow
a teacher to the youth

A preacher on the roof
screaming out
we can all do better!
our desire for destruction
will make sense to me
Never

I think about the places
far off in the face of the furnace
and how the taste of my own freedom
is bitter and nervous

I spit gravel and asphalt
paving the way for future generations
installing these lighthouses
to offer a safe place for salvation

We gather for healing
mend through sound and seance
hoping to resurrect the hope
that these evils pray upon

Let these poems be the specters
of your ancestors' breath
and the reminders
that a movement can only exist
when you choose
                      to
                              take
                                    that
                                          first
                                                  step.

My Love

I met this woman during
my college years—
well-read and comes from
a long line of orators

She is hip-hop, punk and soul
which influence her style
from the head wraps to toe rings—
ripped jeans, black turtlenecks,
thick framed glasses and piercings

Confident yet vulnerable
lured in by her words
assured this was love
butterflies and goosebumps
every time I was in her presence

New York born and bred
raised with the African Beat
instilled within her bones

Wasn't the type to stay still
she moved around
had a residency up in Chi town,
showed out like So What!
became the competitive type
spending much of her time in
smokey bars and cafés

Took trips out west
got in good with the hippies and junkies
the beat always within her
so it was only right
she'd get down with the jazz cats
and my God—
they worked beautifully together

Style evolved and found success
amongst thriving hip-hop scenes
hung around rappers and singers
fitting right in
she was now televised
even found her way into film
getting a taste of that Hollywood life

Always enamored how she
welcomed everyone with open arms
represented the marginalized
and pride communities well

She made it overseas where
she was well received

Younger kids started taking
more notice of her presence
showed them how to find
bravery through their voice

Honored on stages nationally
the youth upholding her essence
I seen it with my own eyes
back in Washington DC

She writes bloody in
Austin, Texas
not afraid to dig deep
and speak truth to light;
some might describe her
cute as a Button in Minneapolis
but don't get it twisted
if there's a cause
she's always down to fight

"Write About Now" she still makes
her way around college campuses
Ted Talk stages
even found success
on *Americas Got Talent*

It's like she hasn't aged a bit
caught her second wind
and now you can see her
at the Grammys
celebrating wins

My love has come a long way

She helped me find my voice
but more importantly my family
she is what defines me
what gives me purpose
where this confidence stems from

Without her
I'm not sure where I'd be
certainly not here
we know these tears too well
we talk about pain often
sharing secrets under covers

reminiscing over bowls of kush
making love in the late hours
of night to jazz records
always enough to put me
in a sentimental mood

She, my vehicle on this journey
never quite sure where
we are heading
but I trust the current
of her collective breath
the strength in her wisdom
and the alchemy of her words

She is all that that flows
through me
mind, body, soul
she is my reflection
my light
She is nothing but poetry

Coley Whisman

Rebuttal to Your Salty Love Poem

What does it mean when I say I love you?
It means even when I don't agree,
when your opinions create friction in my brain,
and weird, constipated looks on my face
I'll listen, ask questions and
try my best to understand.

It means I care about what you're doing.
I'll show up with my atrocious timing
on your first day at your new job
to support you.

It means I think too much about how you're feeling,
whether you have bandwidth or not
to deal with my nonsense.

It doesn't mean my disaster of a junk drawer
won't ever spill out
into your already crowded and stressful day,
but it does mean
I don't want it to.

I'll celebrate your successes
like when you have a shit day at work
and even though they have to write you up,
your superiors, rather than expressing disappointment,
shower you with reassurance and affection
because they love you
and appreciate having you around.

When the world feels like too much,
I'll give what you need most.
Someone to listen or hold you
or more often, space and time to compost.

It means when you finally decide my unskillful knots
that torture your once strong pigeon feet
have become too much to bear,
and you tell me this pain isn't worth it,
I'll understand.

And when you find someone new,
I'll let you complain to me
about how annoying she is,
how she drives you crazy in your mind
and in your bed—
I'll listen to your salty love poems about her
and I'll be happy for you.

If you move across the country for this woman,

and she ends up breaking your heart,
I'll fly out there.
Drive you, your art, your books and your cats back home.
We'll take the Southern Route
and frighten people with our queerness.
I'll hit curbs with the back tire of the moving truck
at every gas station along the way.

And if by some fucking miracle,
your heart decides to love me too,
I'll take it gratefully and not greedily—
that most precious gift.

I'll do my best to make your days easier.
I'll cherish your freedom as much as you.
I'll honor your need to be a god damn feral feline
who sometimes scares people.
Even though I'm an aggressively friendly mutt
of a domesticated dog.
I'll learn how you like your coffee—
Turkish with maple syrup—
and how all of your fucking buttons work.

I'll learn your rhythms and pace
when you need closeness,
and when you need space,
I'll eventually learn to crash into your energy
with less force and more grace.

You suggested me saying *I love you*
was a way to quell my fear.
Well, that is false,
the exact opposite
of what is actually happening here.
Opening to you
heightens my sense of danger a million-fold.
I have panic attacks.
Sometimes the anxiety seems impossible to hold.

Waiting for this bruising of my heart
to end in one devastating rip,
scares me so much
I think about jumping ship
and swimming to solid ground
at least once a week.

What's in it for me? You ask
Sometimes I don't know
but you shine so brightly
I feel grateful
just to be in your orbit,
to occasionally be part of your flow.

I open to you and trust you
because it's true in my soul
that you are one of those people
I am meant to know

I'm supposed to learn from you
and you from me
because…
we challenge each other.

We understand one another in a weird
supportive, combative, affectionate,
annoyed kind of way.
We have more resilience and patience
with each other than we do
with much of the world or ourselves.
We're willing to go
into the uncomfortable places together.

It's not about you,
or about me.
It's about us.

Jesse James Ziegler

Squint
for Andrea

Nothing can dim the light that shines from within.
— Maya Angelou

What would you tell me first if you had to tell me everything?

If you stare directly at the sun,
however briefly, squinting to blur the edges
of the light and warmth that it holds,
you may even convince yourself
that you can absorb pure love
without going blind or being ruined by it.

Yet isn't knowing something to be true,
even with our eyes closed,
and being completely undone by it,
sufficient proof that we stood
in its presence
close enough to feel it in every fiber of our body,
yet somehow living to tell the tale,
built rather than destroyed.

I squint to blur the sharp edges,
see the differences in softer hues,
remind myself that I'm limited by my own vision.
The world really is small and round after all.
I squint to look serious when I'm trying not to cry,
but then I remember trying not to cry
is a sign of weakness,
and I allow the village to draw from the well.

I squint at the fine print, the liner notes and
the distant friends on the horizon,
the ones visiting after a long time
who are just now within view,
and the dearly departed ones
who are just about out of sight,
until we meet again.

Our vision can be permanently altered.
We can collapse to the ground,
as if by melting
and be reformed.
Repurposed into something entirely new,
able to see the sunrises and sunsets
for what they really are,
hellos and goodbyes,
fresh starts and wiping the slate.
What we do between the two
is up to us.
What you do with the two
is up to you.

Shine in the pain and the pleasure,
in the doubt and the daring,
the grief and the gratitude,
loss and love.

Shine like the loneliest heart at Carnival,
newly softened and warmed over
by the song it just heard.

Shine like a glittery Pegasus
with a diamond tipped unicorn horn,
flying beside a comet
over the nebulous neon noise of
the Las Vegas Strip on New Year's Eve.

Shine like the vibrant tableau of lit candles,
celebrating the transparently thin veil
between life and death, all across Oaxaca,
blending with the sacred stars
from a boundless bucolic bird's eye view,
on Dia de Los Muertos.

Shine like the unexpecting eyes
of a Transylvanian youth,
visiting Paris for the very first time,
sinking their tastebuds into their very first bite
of whipped cream and Nutella crepe
at midnight,
right when the Eiffel Tower is set ablaze.

Shine so bright when you're walking
down the street in Tehran, and
someone compliments your glow,
you can turn to them and simply say
It is your eyes that are beautiful
because that may well be
the fiercest response
to a compliment of all time.

Shine like lightening lavishly living in a lighthouse
on the coast of Maine
helping wayward ships find their way safely to shore.
Then give those vessels the grit and grace
to go back out again in the storm.

Shine so purely and unobstructedly
when you walk in a room it
makes others squint,
giving them both the permission and courage
to trust the same light they still have within them.
What would I say first if I had to tell you everything?
Shine like you were made to,
like you're supposed to.
You were born on purpose
for a purpose.

For whether you're coming or going
you're part of me now, so
you're never further off
than my horizon,
you feel closer
with every breath
and I can see you, if
I squint.

Keep

Keep it simple.
Keep writing, keep reading,
keep fighting, keep pleading,
keep lighting and keep leading.
Keep your heart open and your mind aware
Keep coming back for more.
Keep going, keep giving, keep doing.
Keep daring to believe
in a better way of living.
Keep loving and creating.
Keep each other sheltered, sound and warm.
Keep being sanctuary in the storm.
Keep being true to form.
Keep it together, but don't forget
to keep it loose too.
Keep getting home safe.
Keep it real, and keep the faith.
I love you.
Goodbye for now.

Afterword

When my wife and I moved to Carson City from Los Angeles at the start of 2024, I left behind more than just the city I grew up in—but also a poetry family that had seen me grow over the course of twenty years into the poet and publisher I am today. It was difficult to leave that familiarity behind. To not see that family every week at a reading, at a workshop, at a neighborhood coffee shop, at a bar...

I met Jesse at the Mark Twain Festival just a few months after having moved here. My wife and I were staying with her parents while we saved up for a house, and they lived down the street from the Brewery Arts Center where the festival was being held. I had serendipitously wandered in a week or so before the event and began a conversation with the Center and they invited me to have a table at the event and perform. Jesse, being the emcee for the program, introduced himself to me immediately and I was impressed by his professionalism, his personability, and his passion to put the poetry of others before himself. Here was a community leader that was kindred spirit. Here was a poet that defines *real* poetry—a promise to champion the people of a community and not their own ego. We shared origin stories and mission statements, pleasantries and gratefulness—and at the end of the event he told me about Monday Night Poetry at Shim's Tavern that he hosted every Monday night and invited me to check it out. I said, *I would.*

I didn't. Not at first.

I followed his account on Instagram, saw how after every Monday night, he'd post recaps of the prior night's revelries. It looked fantastic, but I just didn't really feel ready to dive into new waters—to be that stranger sitting in the corner. I know that might sound silly. You might think—with my accomplishments—what would I have to be insecure about in a crowd of strangers? Well, I am a poet, after all—at my best, I'm weird and socially awkward.

Anyhow, I finally decided to check out the reading eight months later, on what turned out to be the very night it was celebrating its third anniversary. The place was packed and the people electrifying. I knew right then and there I had found something special, a community I wanted—needed—to be a part of. I hadn't realized how much I missed that feeling of belonging.

After a couple of Mondays, I began to see this was a gathering of voices that celebrated one another on and off the stage. A collective of people who, for a couple of hours once a week, shared in more than just their words, but a microcosm of "nothing can touch us when we're inside these walls," and "we are safe here." *You are safe here.*

It was then I decided that *this* was something special—that this was lightning worth catching in a bottle. I told Jesse I wanted to gift him, and all the poets who have ever shared their words at Shim's on a Monday night, this book. Every person that gets up behind that microphone deserves to have a piece of them exist beyond that stage.

I want to thank Jesse for trusting me with this task. Thank you, Mackensi, for your instrumental aid in putting this collection together. Much thanks, Rachel, for the beautiful cover. Thank you all who have embraced this LA transplant. And lastly, I am so grateful for all the new friendships I have made since finally finding the courage to walk through those doors.

This book is for you. And you. And you. Its lightning, *all* of yours.

— Eric Morago
Publisher, Moon Tide Press

About the Editors

Jesse James Ziegler is Poet Laureate Emeritus for the City of Reno. He is the Vice President of Spoken Views Collective, Creative Director of Monday Night Poetry, True Colors Poetry and Collective Breath Poetry Book Club. He is the communications liaison for the Nevada chapter of the National Federation of State Poetry Societies. He opened and hosted the world premieres of Brandon Leake's original spoken word play Insomnia (Winner of Season 15 AGT). His work has been published by Nevada Humanities, Moon Tide Press, The Bruka Theatre of the Sierra, The Mill Valley Literary Review, Strophes, Black Rock Press and Multnomah University Press.

Mackensi Green, originally from Southeast Texas, is a poet, boulderer, and associate editor for Moon Tide Press. Her work has appeared in *Blue Unicorn* and the *Brushfire Literature and Arts Journal*. She is a current MFA student in Poetry at NYU.

Eric Morago is a multiple Pushcart Prize nominated poet who believes performance carries as much importance on the page as it does off. He is the author of *What We Ache For* and *Feasting on Sky*. Currently Eric teaches writing workshops and is editor-in-chief and publisher of Moon Tide Press and *Spillway Magazine*. He has an MFA in Creative Writing from California State University, Long Beach, and lives in Carson City, Nevada with his wife and four dogs (and probably more someday…dogs, not wives).

Also Available from Moon Tide Press

The Elephant of Surprise, Charles Harper Webb (2025)
Outliving Michael, Steven Reigns (2025)
Prayers with a Side of Cash, Kathleen Florence (2025)
Somewhere, a Playground, Rich Ferguson (2025)
The Tautology of Water, Giovanni Boskovich (2025)
Take Care, Mark Danowsky (2025)
Dilapitatia, Kelly Gray (2025)
Reluctant Prophets, J.D. Isip (2025)
Enormous Blue Umbrella, Donna Hilbert (2025)
Sky Leaning Toward Winter, Terri Niccum (2024)
Living the Sundown: A Caregiving Memoir, G. Murray Thomas (2024)
Figure Study, Kathryn de Lancellotti (2024)
Suffer for This: Love, Sex, Marriage, & Rock 'N' Roll,
    Victor D. Infante (2024)
What Blooms in the Dark, Emily J. Mundy (2024)
Fable, Bryn Wickerd (2024)
Diamond Bars 2, David A. Romero (2024)
Safe Handling, Rebecca Evans (2024)
More Jerkumstances: New & Selected Poems, Barbara Eknoian (2024)
Dissection Day, Ally McGregor (2023)
He's a Color Until He's Not, Christian Hanz Lozada (2023)
The Language of Fractions, Nicelle Davis (2023)
Paradise Anonymous, Oriana Ivy (2023)
Now You Are a Missing Person, Susan Hayden (2023)
Maze Mouth, Brian Sonia-Wallace (2023)
Tangled by Blood, Rebecca Evans (2023)
Another Way of Loving Death, Jeremy Ra (2023)
Kissing the Wound, J.D. Isip (2023)
Feed It to the River, Terhi K. Cherry (2022)
*Beat Not Beat: An Anthology of California Poets Screwing
    on the Beat and Post-Beat Tradition* (2022)
*When There Are Nine: Poems Celebrating the Life and
    Achievements of Ruth Bader Ginsburg* (2022)
The Knife Thrower's Daughter, Terri Niccum (2022)
2 Revere Place, Aruni Wijesinghe (2022)
Here Go the Knives, Kelsey Bryan-Zwick (2022)

Trumpets in the Sky, Jerry Garcia (2022)
Threnody, Donna Hilbert (2022)
A Burning Lake of Paper Suns, Ellen Webre (2021)
Instructions for an Animal Body, Kelly Gray (2021)
Head *V* Heart: New & Selected Poems, Rob Sturma (2021)
Sh!t Men Say to Me: A Poetry Anthology in Response to Toxic Masculinity (2021)
Flower Grand First, Gustavo Hernandez (2021)
Everything is Radiant Between the Hates, Rich Ferguson (2020)
When the Pain Starts: Poetry as Sequential Art, Alan Passman (2020)
This Place Could Be Haunted If I Didn't Believe in Love, Lincoln McElwee (2020)
Impossible Thirst, Kathryn de Lancellotti (2020)
Lullabies for End Times, Jennifer Bradpiece (2020)
Crabgrass World, Robin Axworthy (2020)
Contortionist Tongue, Dania Ayah Alkhouli (2020)
The only thing that makes sense is to grow, Scott Ferry (2020)
Dead Letter Box, Terri Niccum (2019)
Tea and Subtitles: Selected Poems 1999-2019, Michael Miller (2019)
At the Table of the Unknown, Alexandra Umlas (2019)
The Book of Rabbits, Vince Trimboli (2019)
Everything I Write Is a Love Song to the World, David McIntire (2019)
Letters to the Leader, HanaLena Fennel (2019)
Darwin's Garden, Lee Rossi (2019)
Dark Ink: A Poetry Anthology Inspired by Horror (2018)
Drop and Dazzle, Peggy Dobreer (2018)
Junkie Wife, Alexis Rhone Fancher (2018)
The Moon, My Lover, My Mother, & the Dog, Daniel McGinn (2018)
Lullaby of Teeth: An Anthology of Southern California Poetry (2017)
Angels in Seven, Michael Miller (2016)
A Likely Story, Robbi Nester (2014)
Embers on the Stairs, Ruth Bavetta (2014)
The Green of Sunset, John Brantingham (2013)
The Savagery of Bone, Timothy Matthew Perez (2013)
The Silence of Doorways, Sharon Venezio (2013)

Cosmos: An Anthology of Southern California Poetry (2012)
Straws and Shadows, Irena Praitis (2012)
In the Lake of Your Bones, Peggy Dobreer (2012)
I Was Building Up to Something, Susan Davis (2011)
Hopeless Cases, Michael Kramer (2011)
One World, Gail Newman (2011)
What We Ache For, Eric Morago (2010)
Now and Then, Lee Mallory (2009)
Pop Art: An Anthology of Southern California Poetry (2009)
In the Heaven of Never Before, Carine Topal (2008)
A Wild Region, Kate Buckley (2008)
Carving in Bone: An Anthology of Orange County Poetry (2007)
Kindness from a Dark God, Ben Trigg (2007)
A Thin Strand of Lights, Ricki Mandeville (2006)
Sleepyhead Assassins, Mindy Nettifee (2006)
Tide Pools: An Anthology of Orange County Poetry (2006)
Lost American Nights: Lyrics & Poems, Michael Ubaldini (2006)

Patrons

Moon Tide Press would like to thank the following people for their support in helping publish the finest poetry from the Southern California region. To sign up as a patron, visit www.moontidepress.com or send an email to publisher@moontidepress.com.

Anonymous
Robin Axworthy
Conner Brenner
Nicole Connolly
Bill Cushing
Susan Davis
Kristen Baum DeBeasi
Peggy Dobreer
Kate Gale
Dennis Gowans
Alexis Rhone Fancher
HanaLena Fennel
Half Off Books & Brad T. Cox
Donna Hilbert
Jim & Vicky Hoggatt
Michael Kramer
Ron Koertge & Bianca Richards
Gary Jacobelly
Ray & Christi Lacoste

Jeffery Lewis
Zachary & Tammy Locklin
Lincoln McElwee
David McIntire
José Enrique Medina
Michael Miller & Rachanee Srisavasdi
Michelle & Robert Miller
Ronny & Richard Morago
Terri Niccum
Andrew November
Jeremy Ra
Luke & Mia Salazar
Jennifer Smith
Roger Sponder
Andrew Turner
Rex Wilder
Mariano Zaro
Wes Bryan Zwick

www.ingramcontent.com/pod-product-compliance
Lightning Source LLC
Chambersburg PA
CBHW031321160426
43196CB00007B/613